cooking
for
gracie

cooking for gracie

THE MAKING OF A PARENT FROM SCRATCH

KEITH DIXON

CROWN PUBLISHERS
NEW YORK

Portions of this book, along with their accompanying recipes, originally
appeared in slightly different form in *The New York Times:*

"Racket in the Kitchen, Ruckus in the Crib," from *The New York Times*,
© February 27, 2008 *The New York Times*. All rights reserved. Used by
permission and protected by the Copyright Laws of the United States.
The printing, copying, redistribution, or retransmission of the Material
without express written permission is prohibited.

"Momma, I'll Have Some of Whatever You're Having," from *The New York
Times*, © October 1, 2008 *The New York Times*. All rights reserved. Used
by permission and protected by the Copyright Laws of the United States.
The printing, copying, redistribution, or retransmission of the Material
without express written permission is prohibited.

"Drinks to Leave You Laid Back, Not Laid Out," from *The New York
Times*, © March 4, 2009 *The New York Times*. All rights reserved. Used
by permission and protected by the Copyright Laws of the United States.
The printing, copying, redistribution, or retransmission of the Material
without express written permission is prohibited.

Library of Congress Cataloging-in-Publication Data is available on request

ISBN 978-0-307-59187-6
eISBN 978-0-307-59189-0

Printed in the United States of America

Book design by Elina D. Nudelman
Jacket design by Jean Traina
Jacket photographs © Sang An

10 9 8 7 6 5 4 3 2 1

First Edition

For my mother and father

Special thanks to Ellen Levine,
who kept going long after others had given up

CONTENTS

INTRODUCTION

I am what is classically labeled, in domestic circles, "an accident"—a *whoops* and *oops* and *look what the stork brought* surprise of the highest order. My parents are altogether upbeat about this. In fact, my father once reminded me that it's the things that *don't* turn out the way you expect that make life worth living. Still, whenever I reflect on my accidental status, I can't help picturing my mother standing with the phone pressed to her ear, two boys already raging around the apartment, a trembling hand lightly touching her brow as the doctor delivers the results of the pregnancy test.

Symmetrically, my daughter, Gracie, also didn't arrive according to plan—or rather, she didn't arrive according to the plan my wife, Jessica, and I had formulated. Instead, Gracie showed up according to her plan—which is to say that she showed up five weeks early and at about half the weight one would expect for a new baby. Her abrupt arrival foretold other unexpected shocks, a chain of surprises involving Gracie's eating, her teeth, our sleep. I've always been a cooking fiend, someone who spends as much of his free time as possible at the chopping block and burner, so it's no surprise that many of these changes first made themselves known in the kitchen. Appropriately, it was the skills I refined in the kitchen as I began to cook for my daughter that helped me meet the challenges that took place outside the kitchen. Some of these skills related to advance planning, but for the most part they were about learning to acclimatize quickly to the unexpected—I learned to adapt in the kitchen; then, by extension, I learned to adapt elsewhere. When I look back on my first year as a parent, everything about it seems to tie in to cooking for Gracie.

(To be sure, not all of the recipes here are what new parents— those marathoners, those Iron Men of the witching hour—want to tackle when they finally have a free moment. Rest assured there are plenty of simpler recipes inside—in the November chapter, for example, and the December chapter, which has a recipe with only five ingredients [two of which are salt and pepper] and the September chapter, which has simple grilling recipes— that were engineered to yield the greatest amount of satisfaction with the least amount of effort. If I seem a little naive for offering up a recipe for a three-hour braised short rib, well, I am. For people like me, especially in regard to the kitchen, less is never more. For people like me, only *more* is more. It's my hope that the tired reader who just wants something to eat, and the less hassle the better, will forgive me these ten-step epics and will instead flip to some of those less demanding recipes.)

A few of the chapters herein were first published in the *New York Times*—as I was writing them I thought they were just simple food pieces offering kitchen tips to other enthusiastic home cooks struggling against the challenges of cooking with and for a child. But around the time of my daughter's first birthday, I began to realize that maybe there was a unifying idea to be found there, a singularity that applied to something more wide reaching than a newspaper article.

This book ends with all three principals happy and healthy— which means it's a success story. But it begins with the narrator in a state of relative crisis, as any responsible book should. Too, it begins at night, because a real crisis always takes place after nightfall, and the later the better. The narrator has just realized that life no longer operates according to his schedule and that the kitchen may offer clues on how best to adapt.

My past informs this present. For stated reasons, I have a solemn appreciation for the experience to be gained when life sweeps parents away into something that isn't quite what they'd planned. It would be nice if there were more accidents like these up ahead. I bet they'll give me some good stories to tell.

cooking for gracie

OCTOBER

famished

Just weeks into the experience of parenthood, I seem to experience a fresh epiphany about every other day—*moments of clarity,* addicts call them, in which the camera lens of life is screwed sharply into focus and the afflicted suddenly realizes what path he must take.

I'm having a moment of clarity now, alone here in my kitchen at night, where I'm spooning and spooning cold cereal. This is dinner these days: standing at the kitchen window with a bowl of breakfast. I'm nettled by problems with sleep, and with tim-ing, and with other things. The hour is late enough that even the pointillist panorama of New York, a city I've called home for fifteen years, seems almost subdued; York Avenue, five stories below, is nearly deserted, and taxis streak by only occasionally. Summer is barely hanging on, having exhausted itself with hot September. The scene appears tranquil to the naked eye, but it's really not—if this kitchen were the galley of a Boeing jet, the FASTEN SEAT BELTS sign would be blinking right now, directing all passengers to buckle up and prepare for *terrible turbulence.* I've ruined dinner, blackened it to the pan—the haze hanging below the ceiling is the proof. My wife, Jessica, and I were going to eat six pristine lamb chops an hour ago, but as we sat down at the table our weeks-old daughter, Grace, gave a cry of hunger from her room—and I looked up with the troubled expression of a picnicker who hears distant thunder.

Just weeks in, and I'm already a worried dad. The big questions seek me out after midnight and apprehend me at the moment of sleep. There in the night I face down my fears about Gracie's low birth weight and, one at a time, put them in the proper perspective—the next morning, though, the fears are always somehow revived, renewed, reinvigorated. Our daughter was born light, far too light, and whenever she delivers a cry of hunger we snap to attention. So an hour ago we abandoned dinner, and just now I blackened the chops trying to reheat them. I'd thought this would be a simple process of applying the flame, the necessary heat, but things moved much faster than I expected and quickly evolved into a Larry, Moe, and Curly scene of the highest order. As I heaved the window open, fanning the smoke out into the night, I wondered if it was possible to be mad at a kitchen implement. But no, it's hunger itself that I'm mad at—I was hungry for those chops, and now I'm having a bowl of breakfast instead. There was a time when I thought of hunger as a useful, instructive thing—not just physical hunger but hunger for things like success or romantic love. The idea was that the wanting could teach you things about yourself, about your various prowling appetites, and perhaps I was right in that, because tonight's hunger has propelled me into a *moment of clarity*, with all of its dreadful data about my situation.

Here is what I'm slowly coming to understand: What is broken in the kitchen is broken elsewhere—the problem would appear to be that life no longer moves according to my schedule. If you're a writer or a cook, timing is crucial; if you happen to be both, as I am, you're finished without it. I used to have it, this timing, in the kitchen and on the page, but now it's gone. I'm a beat behind in everything I do—I go around half the time feeling like an actor who belongs in a drama and finds himself instead in a comedy, where the jokes are all at his expense.

I've felt this way for weeks—since September 9, 2007, when I surfaced from a deep sleep around 4 a.m. and found Jessica standing over me in the pale bedside light. Marriage has taught me a few things, among them that you should be worried when your pregnant wife wakes you at 4 a.m. by standing over you with the lights already on.

My confusion resolved itself quickly enough when Jessica told me in no uncertain terms that she hadn't slept one minute all night and added that she was pretty sure our baby was on the way, showing me startling evidence to the same. (I'll not describe it here but rather note that the condition "bloody show" is very well named indeed, and as bracing as two strong cups of coffee to see. Google it.) I slapped around on the floor for about ten minutes, searching for my clothes, and we phoned the obstetrician. The baby, if she came today, would be five weeks early. At our latest sonogram we were told that the baby's weight was just north of four pounds. In most cases an obstetrician encourages a couple to remain at home until the woman is through early labor, but the fact that we were five weeks early, combined with other unusual conditions of the pregnancy, was enough to cause him to tell us to come on in, and right away. There were no cars out so early—we hunted down a cab, and the driver seemed to understand everything with a glance. He thundered through intersection and along crosscut, around hairpin and down avenue. Jessica was in that trancelike state women achieve when the biological imperative asserts itself; that is, she was an arresting example of female can-do. If there'd been any time to stop and think, I suppose I would have panicked, but I was fully occupied by the events unfolding around me, and anyway, I was still shaking off the anesthetic effects of the martini I'd had at dinner the night before. We swept past the sleepy hospital admitting desk and were fired skyward by the express elevator to the birthing floor, where an IV was inserted into the back of Jessica's hand. At this point Jessica's blood pressure swirled upward, and I heard a staffer in attendance use the word *preeclampsia*. A monitor strapped over Jessica's navel, which measured the contractions she was experiencing, began delivering data to a printer beside the bed—this immediately began drawing rolling ocean swells, and for a moment the illusion was complete: I imagined that this was indeed an ocean liner, and here were the heavy seas, with their attendant queasiness. But then the IV began to do its work, Jessica's blood pressure eased, and the printout swells subsided into barely noticeable upticks.

That's it? I asked, and the attending doctor repeated my question in the declarative.

Four brief hours at the hospital, and our fortunes had turned.

During the cab ride home I was electric with the cherry high of someone who has been granted a reprieve—every other block I felt the urge to seize the cabbie by the shoulder and say, "That was a close one, wasn't it?" Now I had time to prepare for this thing I hadn't been prepared for. I helped Jessica into bed, seared a grilled cheese sandwich for her and watched her eat, then pulled the covers up to her chin and drew the curtains. After offering a heartfelt plea that she rest, and rest well, I stepped into the shower.

What a still moment that was, standing blameless beneath the roaring showerhead, nodding to myself, arms crossed, eyes closed, breathing deeply through my nose and reflecting on the near miss of a five-week-premature birth. Close, Keith, I thought, so close, *too close*, and then hollering Jessica ran into the bathroom and leaped, fully dressed and exultant, into the shower with me.

Her water had broken.

The warning shot had revealed itself to be the report of a starting gun.

We stood in silence for a moment—facing each other, hands clasped, like a couple about to recite a marriage vow. Even the most vivid memories tend to fade with time, but decades from now, when Death appears in my doorway and beckons with a bent finger, this is the image that will burn brightly in my mind's eye—Jessica standing fully dressed in the shower, clothes dripping, wet hair plastered to her face and neck, and the waters that had protected Gracie for the first thirty-five weeks of her life now swirling around my bare ankles.

Here comes the future, at 140 heartbeats per minute.

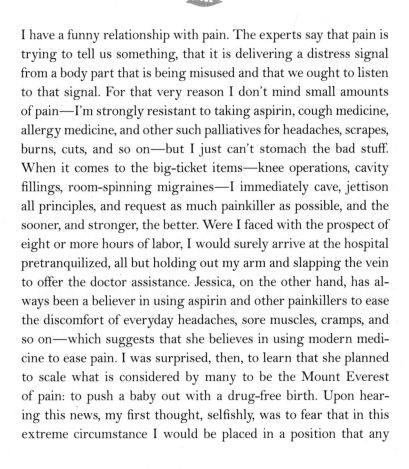

I have a funny relationship with pain. The experts say that pain is trying to tell us something, that it is delivering a distress signal from a body part that is being misused and that we ought to listen to that signal. For that very reason I don't mind small amounts of pain—I'm strongly resistant to taking aspirin, cough medicine, allergy medicine, and other such palliatives for headaches, scrapes, burns, cuts, and so on—but I just can't stomach the bad stuff. When it comes to the big-ticket items—knee operations, cavity fillings, room-spinning migraines—I immediately cave, jettison all principles, and request as much painkiller as possible, and the sooner, and stronger, the better. Were I faced with the prospect of eight or more hours of labor, I would surely arrive at the hospital pretranquilized, all but holding out my arm and slapping the vein to offer the doctor assistance. Jessica, on the other hand, has always been a believer in using aspirin and other painkillers to ease the discomfort of everyday headaches, sore muscles, cramps, and so on—which suggests that she believes in using modern medicine to ease pain. I was surprised, then, to learn that she planned to scale what is considered by many to be the Mount Everest of pain: to push a baby out with a drug-free birth. Upon hearing this news, my first thought, selfishly, was to fear that in this extreme circumstance I would be placed in a position that any

husband deeply dreads: that of feeling essentially useless.* There
were a number of logical fallacies we employed to mitigate my
(and Jessica's) fear about meeting this challenge. "It's temporary,"
she would say, referring to the pain, "it's temporary," and I would
nod my head and say, "Yes, it's temporary," thinking, But, Jessica,
this is a very *long* temporary, lasting hours (or even, God help us,
days) instead of moments. Nevertheless, we stuck with this line of
logic, to great success. "It's temporary," she would say, and I'd nod
my head and repeat the phrase back.

We would discuss this matter of painkillers nightly, sometimes
more than once a night, and we even took a weeks-long class on
how to survive a drug-free delivery.† Through the early stages of
this, there remained an element of unreality about the whole thing,
which helped tamp down the urgency of the discussion. Many first
pregnancies, after all, don't begin to show until some time during
the second trimester, which means that even as you're having these
hard discussions about things like painkillers, the whole enterprise
at times seems almost theoretical, as if you were being rooked by
a slew of doctors and baby-gear vendors trying to separate you
and your wife from your last dollar. The doctors, these men and
women dressed in long white coats, all busily poking columns of
blood test results, a tax audit's worth of facts about height, weight,
bone length, and fetal age, and the occasional sonogram photo-

---

* This turns out to be a position that fathers-to-be find themselves in regularly.
Throughout the many weeks of the pregnancy the father is often, much to his
dismay, reduced to following stage directions—and he finds himself, paradoxically,
in a key role that has virtually no lines.

† And here I didn't exactly earn votes for the title World's Greatest Husband. This
class was important to Jessica, and, precisely because it was so important to her, I
should have attended cheerfully and without complaint and in fact made a point to
tell her that I believed in her and was here to support her—but instead I grumbled
about the quasi-new-age aspects of the class, the paltry snacks on offer for pregnant women who were skipping dinner, the hours-long commitment, and so forth.
In a nicely symmetrical comeuppance, the class turned out to be of great benefit
to me: We had planned to hire a doula to help us through the birth, and when
Gracie arrived early, before we'd had a chance to locate a doula, it was exactly the
practices I learned in this class that allowed me to help Jessica through the delivery.

graph, keep *telling* you that a baby is on the way—but for the first five months you study your wife's belly region and see no obvious evidence that any of this is true.* I remained silent through much of the drug-free delivery classes, thinking, Well, it's her call isn't it? But I also remained silent because a significant part of me believed that this would all resolve itself when the first wave of contractions hit and Jessica, duly startled by the *size* of the pain, raised her hand to call for an epidural and perhaps even a martini on the side to hold her until the anesthesiologist had done her work. I had this opinion because this is the way *I* would have come at the birth—so I was doubly ashamed by my self-assured outlook when Jessica devastated all parties involved by seeing her way through labor without so much as an aspirin to blunt the edge of the contractions, even though near the end of it the pain was so intense and went on for so long that it caused her eyes to roll up until the whites showed and forced her to grip me so tightly about the waist for support that she threw out my back.†

Seemingly all at once, with the fury of a tornado that had gathered for hours and then dropped out of clear blue sky, here was the moment of birth, and here was Gracie, born at four pounds— her skin alarmingly gray. Just seconds old, the obstetrician held my daughter aloft with a single hand, then carried her over to the heat lamp, where an attending staff member rubbed her dry with a towel, her color rising now, the staff member suddenly sweeping past me, taking Gracie out of the room in a cart, things already moving faster, and Jessica didn't bother to remove her oxygen mask

---

* Though I should qualify: Although in the first few months I saw no evidence of the baby in my wife's *belly region,* I did see dramatic evidence that her body was going through remarkable physiological changes, namely, that this author's wife, at the late first-trimester period of pregnancy, suddenly blossomed into a striking *Playboy*-bunnyesque build, one sharply arresting in its perfect recollection of many of this author's latent adolescent desires, but enough about that.
† My pain outlook is surely informed by the fact that I'm the son of a doctor and a trained medical technologist and have a deeply engrained trust in modern medicine and its practitioners.

when she lifted her head and said: "Go with her." Then down the hall, through the double doors and into another wing, this one as harshly lighted as an interrogation room, Plexiglas isolettes lining the walls, each occupied by a tiny baby, and I thought, Ha ha, very funny, joke's over, the NICU is where Other People's children go.

Isn't it?

But I was now Other People, one of those persons whose misfortunes you talk about in hushed tones, and the joke was on me. The unreality of the moment was scored by a sort of electronic symphony, alarms sounded by individual heart rate and blood-oxygen monitors. Gracie now had one around her foot. The alarms are false, a nurse said, grasping my elbow for effect, no need to worry, it just means the baby is shaking the cuff and the machine isn't getting an accurate reading—but later that night another baby's alarm went off, and this time a pair of nurses seemed to materialize out of thin air at either side of the isolette, one with her hand inside going about some sort of complicated business with a baby the size of her palm. When I got it, when I realized what was happening, it was like being dashed with a bucket of cold water: the baby's heart had stopped, or its rate had grown erratic. The nurse was giving it CPR. I watched the nurse bring the baby out of it, my heart in my throat even though it wasn't my kid, and I reflected that if you'd asked me before Gracie had arrived what emotion I thought I would have experienced in such a situation, I probably would have guessed sadness. And I would have guessed wrong. This was something more like waking from a nightmare long after midnight and sensing, with the decisiveness of a hatchet stroke, that someone was in my room and was here to harm me. Except this predatory force wasn't here for me—it was here for my baby, and I could do nothing to protect her.

Three days later I was introduced to a diagnosis known as Failure to Thrive. The parents of its victims may feel inclined to ask why the name must be so literal. Perhaps we should rename hypothermia Failure to Keep Warm. I learned about this condition when my Gracie Failed to Thrive and seemed to waste away before our glazed eyes, her weight sinking below four pounds. First she became too exhausted to eat; then, because she was taking in no nourishment, she became even *more* exhausted, and the situation rapidly deteriorated from there. During the mid-day feeding she was nearly unresponsive, asleep in her mother's arms while all around us babies were crying out for food. I was paralyzed emotionally. It was like trying to feed a plastic doll. The nurse assigned to us, who had hovered at a distance for a day, now moved in, as if cued by a director with very good timing, and with gratitude I felt control being taken away from us. We were told that Gracie would be fed with a tube that night and we were sent home. The last stage of my grandmother's life began when she was fitted with a feeding tube; I was helpless to avoid draw-ing parallels. I found myself thinking, You need to begin dealing with this *now*. You need to accept what may happen. If you don't, this is going to send you all to pieces. You will not recover.

My mother: "It'll be OK. Babies are *tough*." But I'm not. At home, seeking comfort, familiar rhythms, I made dinner with ingredi-ents from the cabinet. It didn't help. *She'll come out of it. You'll see.* Sometimes I'd feel all right, almost human for ten or even twenty seconds, and then I'd picture my three-day-old daughter limp in her mother's arms, unresponsive and seeming to sink toward some lower state of consciousness, and all at once I'd feel as if the ground had vanished beneath me. The fear had somehow got into the air and followed us home; it was something you breathed, something you swam through and confronted anew in each room you fled to.

I watched my wife seek assistance from the usual array of Jessica diversions—the book, the laptop, the phone—but this time she was engaging each of these things with tears streaming down her face. She was terrified, she said, that Gracie would be in pain during the process, and she was distraught that she wouldn't be present to offer comfort. It was my duty, as husband, to be of comfort to Jessica, to mitigate *her* pain. But I was no comfort to anyone now, not even myself. My wife had been crying all night long. But then so had I.

This is how I feel when I fly over water at night.

Which is to say: out of control, beyond the help of a higher power, and reliant on nothing but faith whistled up out of nowhere.

I push the plate of lamb chops aside and set the bowl of cereal on the counter. I'm no longer hungry, not for food, anyway—it's something else I want, something I'm having a hard time identifying. Gracie is hungry, and I'm hungry. She *did* come out of it, just like everyone said she would. Our daughter is home with us, gaining weight—but in many ways I'm still back there in the NICU, a spirit haunting the waiting room.

I snap off the overhead light, then wrap up the chops for a stew I'll make tomorrow and open the refrigerator door—the fluorescent interior light bathes the kitchen surfaces in soothing lunar shades: ultramarine, cerulean, Bondi Blue. I'm tempted to remain here, where things are being shown, if only for a moment, in the kindest light. In a little while I'll have to come up with something for Jessica to eat—I want her to eat well, which will help Gracie get the nourishment she needs.

A simple syllogism that keeps playing its logic in my head:

Major premise: *I'm cooking for Jessica.*
Minor premise: *Gracie gets all her nourishment from Jessica.*
Conclusion: *When I cook for Jessica, I'm cooking for Gracie.*

Eventually Gracie is fed, rocked, and gentled off to sleep, and Jessica joins me. We watch a movie that makes us laugh, but my attention is divided. I realize what it is I'm hungry for. It is a lack of reassurance that has left me famished. But reassurance is in short supply these days, and it will be left to me to supply my own. Caring for my daughter—cooking for her—helps me cope.

And it's becoming increasingly apparent that when I'm cooking for Gracie, I'm caring for myself.

And I'm doing it poorly. In this situation you don't make delicate lamb chops, not if you're wise to the new timing—you make lamb shanks, or braised veal, or short ribs, or a chickpea stew. You make something that can cook away all night, if need be.

I must adapt, or we'll all do without.

Soon I'll have to learn to cook all over again.

Lamb Chops "Scottadito"
Serves 2

I was tempted to make the recipe for 8 chops, but I'm not the biggest fan of cold lamb and prefer not to have leftovers. I devised this recipe after deciding that my old marinade, which included balsamic vinegar and Dijon mustard, was making the chops too heavy, too rich. To remedy that, I moved in the opposite direction, going for the lightening brightness of lemon zest and coriander and adding a pinch of sugar to help the chops form a browned crust during the brief sear.

The dry-rub technique is also used in the Rosemary-Smoked Steak in the September chapter. A dry rub that includes salt is rubbed over the chops; the salt pulls moisture to the surface, where it picks up the flavors of the rub before being drawn back into the chops. Works like a charm.

These chops are at their best exactly 2 minutes after they come out of the pan; they are impossible to reheat, as they overcook almost instantly. I recommend making them only when you're sure dinner won't be interrupted.

> 2 teaspoons freshly ground black pepper
> Zest of 1 lemon

2 teaspoons salt

1 garlic clove

½ teaspoon whole coriander seed

Very big pinch of sugar

3 tablespoons peanut oil or olive oil

6 single-rib lamb chops, the smallest you can
  get your hands on, untrimmed

1. Combine the pepper, lemon zest, salt, garlic, coriander, and sugar in a spice grinder and grind to a fine paste. (If you don't have a spice grinder, just chop and crack all ingredients as finely as possible and then combine.) Slather the dry rub over all surfaces of the chops, and allow the chops to rest on a plate at room temperature for 60 minutes.

2. After the chops have rested, heat a large iron frying pan over the highest heat possible until the pan is extremely hot. Add the oil to the pan and swirl once to coat the pan. When the oil just begins to smoke, gently lay the chops in the pan. Sear for exactly 90 seconds without moving the chops, flip, sear another 90 seconds undisturbed (if you are indeed cooking in a smoking-hot pan, this cooking time will give you very rare chops—add another 45 seconds to 1 minute searing time in total for chops that are cooked to around medium rare), then move the chops to a plate. Allow them to rest for exactly 2 minutes, then bring the resting plate to the table, and have both diners eat the chops directly from the plate with their hands.

Tagliatelle with Braised
Veal and Gremolata Pesto

Serves 2

Like most braises, this recipe is forgiving when it comes to cooking time—the real enemy here is having the oven temperature too high. If the stock and wine are boiling furiously, the finished meat will be dry. Be sure to keep things at a gentle simmer instead.

If you'd like to save some time, skip making the pasta yourself and use store-bought fresh pasta instead.

> 5 tablespoons olive oil
>
> 2 veal shanks (osso bucco), bone in (2 inches thick)
>
> Salt and freshly ground black pepper
>
> 5 garlic cloves, 3 smashed, 2 finely minced
>
> 2 stalks celery, diced
>
> 1 carrot, diced
>
> ½ medium Spanish onion, diced
>
> 1½ cups dry white wine
>
> 1 bay leaf
>
> One 28-ounce can whole peeled tomatoes, juice discarded, tomatoes coarsely chopped
>
> 1 cup chicken stock
>
> ¼ cup finely chopped fresh parsley
>
> Zest of 1 large lemon, finely minced
>
> 6 ounces tagliatelle or other fresh pasta (see Fresh Pasta Dough, page 14) or store-bought fresh pasta

Note: If you want to make the recipe ahead, you can prepare the braised veal through step 4—store the veal shanks immersed in the braising liquid overnight or longer. To finish, bring shanks and braising liquid to a bare simmer in the same pot you used to cook them, then move to step 5.

1. Preheat the oven to 300°F.

2. In a medium braiser or dutch oven, heat 3 tablespoons of the oil over high heat. Season the veal shanks with salt and pepper. When the oil just begins to smoke, lay the veal in the pan and sear until browned on all sides, for 8 to 10 minutes. Remove to a platter.

3. Lower heat to medium. Add 1 tablespoon oil, the 3 smashed

garlic cloves, celery, carrot, and onion to the pan. Sauté until soft and transparent, about 4 minutes. Add the wine, raise heat to high, and boil for 5 minutes to concentrate the liquid and boil off the alcohol. Add the bay leaf and tomatoes, then the stock, and again bring to a boil. Nestle the shanks in the sauce. Cover and place in the oven. Check after 15 minutes. If the sauce is boiling furiously, lower the oven temperature by 15°F. If not simmering at all, raise by 15°F. Repeat checking until sauce is just simmering.

4. Cook for about 2½ hours, until the meat is falling off the bone, occasionally turning and basting the veal shanks.

5. While the osso bucco is finishing its braise, bring a large pot of salted water to a boil over high heat. In a small bowl, combine the parsley, lemon zest, remaining 1 tablespoon of the oil, and 2 minced garlic cloves and combine well. Season with salt and pepper.

6. When the osso bucco has finished braising, remove the shanks from the braising liquid and set on a plate. Add the tagliatelle to the boiling water and cook until the pasta is tender but still has some bite—about 5 minutes. Drain the tagliatelle and stir into the braising liquid. Separate the lobes of meat from the bone with your hands or two spoons, discarding any overly fatty pieces and connective tissue, then add the meat to the pasta and combine well. (If dinner is delayed, allow the pasta to cool down in the pan. To reheat, add a splash of stock and a tablespoon of unsalted butter and warm over a low flame, stirring to moisten.) After plating, sprinkle the parsley-zest mixture over pasta. Serve immediately.

Fresh Pasta Dough
Serves 3 to 4

This recipe is included not so much for its ingredient combination, which can be found in a thousand slightly varied iterations from as many sources, but for the information on how to (1) make it in the food processor rather than laboriously knead by hand; (2) roll it out and slice it by hand, which is actually easier than using a pasta machine; and (3) use the freezer to quickly set the pasta before storing it. I've tried letting freshly made pasta dry in the open air, but the results often shatter to pieces before I can safely store them.

If you decide to make a double recipe, do step 1 in two separate batches—most food processors can't handle the 3½ cups of flour a double batch requires and will conk out midrecipe.

All-purpose flour gives fine results here, though when I can get my hands on it I like to use Caputo's red-bag Chef's Flour, a Tipo 00 flour with a gluten content up around 12 percent—it yields a terrific bite (you can order it online at fornobravo.com).

> 1¾ cups all-purpose flour or Tipo 00 flour
>
> 3 small to medium eggs
>
> ¼ teaspoon extra virgin olive oil

1. Add the flour to a food processor fitted with the dough blade. Lightly beat the eggs and olive oil in a bowl, then add to the food processor. Pulse the dough five or six times until it begins to come together into a ball (it's OK if there's a little loose flour around the edges of the bowl), then turn on the processor to knead the dough for exactly 60 seconds. (During the kneading process, the dough will pick up most of the loose flour around the edges of the bowl and form into a ball. If the dough refuses to form into a ball, add flour 1 tablespoon at a time, restarting the machine each time, until the dough forms a ball. You shouldn't need more than 2 cups total.)

2. Turn the dough out onto a lightly floured surface and knead with your hands until the dough is smooth and elastic, about 30 seconds. Form into a ball, wrap in plastic wrap, and leave at room temperature for 30 minutes.

3. After the dough has rested, halve it. Wrap one of the halves back in the plastic wrap, then roll out the other half as thinly as possible—if

you roll it out as thinly as you should, you'll get a 15 × 15-inch irregularly shaped square. When you begin rolling it out, it may at first easily spread out, then contract a bit—keep at it, and eventually the dough will relax and roll out. After the dough is rolled out thinly, flour the top of the dough lightly, roll it up as you would roll a rug, and cut the dough into whatever width strand you desire. (To make tagliatelle, for example, slice the roll into ¼-inch ribbons.)

4. After you've sliced the entire roll, pick up a few of the slices and shake them around to open them into a loose, messy handful of strands. Repeat with remaining slices until all are gathered in a loose, messy pile. Place the pile on a lightly floured plate in the freezer. Repeat with remaining plastic-wrapped dough, freezing the resulting pasta after it's been sliced. You can bring this dough directly from the plate in the freezer to the boiling water for cooking. Or bag up the pasta in a zip-lock bag and leave it in the freezer until it's time to cook.

Short Ribs with Carrot-Rosemary Puree
Serves 2 (including some first-rate leftovers)

A classic pairing of braised beef with carrots, the carrots assuming a role on the plate usually given to mashed potatoes.

> 3 tablespoons extra virgin olive oil
> 2½ pounds beef short ribs, bone in, trimmed of excess fat
> Salt and freshly ground black pepper
> 1 cup each coarsely chopped onion, carrot, celery, mushroom
> 2 tablespoons tomato paste
> 1 bottle dry red wine
> 4 sprigs fresh thyme

> 3 to 4 cups beef stock
>
> 6 medium carrots, sliced into 2-inch lengths
> (about 2½ cups total)
>
> ½ small onion
>
> 2 medium sprigs fresh rosemary, woody stem discarded

Note: If you want to make the recipe ahead, you can prepare the short ribs and carrots through step 6. Refrigerate the short ribs immersed in the braising liquid overnight or longer.

1. Preheat the oven to 300°F.

2. Heat the oil in a medium dutch oven or ovenproof stock pot over high heat. Season the short ribs well with salt and pepper. When the oil just begins to smoke, add the short ribs, meaty side down. Brown well on all sides, about 10 minutes total. Set the short ribs aside on a plate.

3. Lower the heat to medium. Add the vegetables to the pot and sauté until softened, about 4 minutes, and season with salt and pepper. Add the tomato paste and sauté for an additional minute. Pour in the bottle of wine and add 2 of the thyme sprigs and raise the heat to high. Boil the wine until reduced by half, about 20 minutes.

4. Lay the short ribs in the wine, bone side down, nestling them amid the vegetables, and add just enough stock to cover the ribs—if you've added all the stock and the ribs still aren't submerged, add some water to submerge them. Bring to a boil, cover pot, and slide into oven. Check after 15 minutes. If the sauce is boiling furiously, lower the oven temperature by 15°F. If not simmering at all, raise by 15°F. Continue checking until the sauce is just simmering.

5. After the ribs are in the oven, make the carrot puree: Add the carrots, onion, rosemary, salt and pepper and enough water to cover the carrots and bring to a boil over high heat. Lower the heat and simmer the carrots for 15 minutes. Transfer the carrots, onion, and rosemary and 1/3 cup of the cooking liquid to a blender and puree until smooth. Transfer to a bowl, cover with plastic wrap, and refrigerate.

6. Braise the ribs for 2½ hours, until the meat is tender and falling off the bone. Remove the pot from oven. Move the short ribs with bones to a plate, then gently slice the short rib meat away from any bones still adhering, cutting away any connective tissue. Discard the bones and connective tissue. Strain the braising liquid, discard the vegetables, and use a fat skimmer or a large spoon to defat the surface of the liquid. Return the liquid to the pot. Place the pot over high heat and reduce the braising liquid for 20 minutes at a full boil to thicken the sauce, then turn off the heat. Lay the short ribs back in sauce and cover the pot to keep warm.

7. (If you've refrigerated the short ribs overnight, take the container out of the refrigerator and skim and discard the fat that has hardened on the surface of the liquid with a spoon.) When ready to eat, turn the flame under the short ribs to medium-low and bring the cooking liquid to the barest simmer. (If dinner is delayed, just turn the flame off and rewarm when ready.) Pour the carrot puree into a small saucepan and gently warm over low heat. When the carrots and short ribs are warm, place a portion of the carrot puree in the middle of a plate. Rest a short rib or two on top of the puree. Spoon the reduced short rib sauce all around. Top the short rib with a thyme sprig for garnish. Repeat with a second plate and serve immediately.

Chickpea Minestra with
Fennel Salad and Chive Oil

Serves 3 to 4

If you don't love the licorice flavor of fennel, you could skip the fennel salad altogether—or you could substitute a last-minute swirl of basil puree (*see step 1 of Provençal Soup with Basil Puree on page 51*).

FOR THE CHIVE OIL

½ cup extra virgin olive oil

Bunch of chives

FOR THE FENNEL SALAD

1 medium fennel bulb, cored, tough outer stalks peeled and discarded, and finely diced, wispy tops reserved

1 tablespoon minced chives

2 tablespoons minced shallot

2 tablespoons extra virgin olive oil

Salt and freshly ground black pepper

FOR THE MINESTRA

2 tablespoons extra virgin olive oil, plus more for drizzling

1 slice bacon

2 stalks celery, diced

2 medium carrots, diced

1 large Spanish onion, diced

1 teaspoon minced fresh rosemary

4 cups canned chickpeas, rinsed and drained

1 teaspoon crushed red pepper flakes

2 sprigs fresh parsley

2 bay leaves

Salt and freshly ground black pepper

½ cup dry white wine

2 cups chicken stock

Rind of 1 wedge of Parmesan or pecorino cheese

Note: if you want to make this recipe ahead, complete the recipe through step 5, then refrigerate the individual ingredients. To serve, reheat the minestra, then complete step 6.

1. *Make the chive oil:* Place the oil and chives in a blender and puree. Set aside to rest at room temperature.

2. *Make the fennel salad:* Combine the fennel, chives, shallot, wispy fennel tops, and oil in a mixing bowl and stir. Season with salt and pepper and allow to rest at room temperature.

3. *Make the minestra:* Heat 2 tablespoons of oil over medium heat in a large saucepan or medium dutch oven and add the bacon slice. Allow the bacon to crisp and render its fat, turning a few times, 6 to 8 minutes. Discard the bacon slice and add the celery, carrots, and onion and sauté, stirring regularly, until soft, for 5 minutes. Add rosemary, chickpeas, pepper flakes, parsley, and bay leaves and combine well. Season with salt and pepper and then add the wine and stock and enough cold water to cover the chickpeas by 2 inches. Bring to a simmer, add the cheese rind, cover, and lower heat to medium-low. Simmer for 60 minutes to allow the flavors to mingle.

4. Remove the cheese rind, bay leaves, and parsley sprigs from the minestra and discard. Remove 2 cups of the vegetables from the minestra, leaving the liquid behind, and set the vegetables aside in a bowl. Using an immersion blender or regular blender, puree the remaining minestra—if using a regular blender, place a kitchen towel over the lid to make sure hot liquid doesn't splatter, then pour the puree back into the dutch oven. Pour the reserved vegetables back into the minestra—it will be quite thick. Keep warm over a medium-low flame.

5. Strain the chive oil through a fine-mesh sieve, saving the olive oil. Discard the chive solids.

6. Ladle the minestra into individual bowls. Stir the fennel salad again with your hands, then gently place a small handful of the fennel salad in the center of each serving of minestra. Spoon a line of the chive oil around the perimeter of the soup and serve.

horror show

November has arrived. Apparently it brought weather from London along with it. When I look out the window, what do I see? People running to get out of the weather. Below, scissoring suits and trench coats leap over puddles, over torrents of gutters, some using a tented tabloid as shelter, some wrestling umbrellas that have been inverted by a fugitive updraft of wind. This is a difficult time for everyone here in New York, we who must walk nearly everywhere we go and line up outside while waiting for our seat in the humid locker of the crosstown bus.

Improbably, Jessica and I are the parents of a two-month-old. Somewhere along the line I blinked, and eight weeks whipped by. Despite the quick passage of the past months, a curious time inversion, a time contradiction, has established itself, in which the weeks scroll away behind us but the days lag and fragment. These days a week seems to pass by in about a minute. But every minute seems to drag on for about a week.

This is because of sleep—or rather, it's because of the sleep we want but are no longer getting. Exhaustion tells us that we're *really in this*, that we're really doing this: parenting an infant. I find evidence of this role change every time I approach a mirror, expecting to encounter my own image, and instead meet a vampire in the glass. This impression is helped along by the uniform I wear: dark blues and blacks in the swirling, yielding fabrics of the infirm, clothes that go on and come off easily, especially in the middle of the night, and I keep the hood of my sweatshirt always raised against the cold.

The notion of our long-term commitment is sinking in. If October was a month of adrenaline, of rising every morning to the fated challenges of a big day, November is a month of identifying with a suffering marathoner: one who has about twenty miles to go and already finds his limbs sending up messages of pain. Halloween passed a few days ago, but rainy November provides the true horror show.

In my previous life, sleep was eight uninterrupted hours every night plus one serious sleep-in session per weekend plus a nap smuggled here or there. Good-bye to all that. Good-bye, good-bye. Now sleep is an all-day crash course of twelve-second catnaps and two-minute nod-offs and three-hour dreamless comas that never quite meet the collective need. I used to roll and twitch and sleepwalk all night long—I used to exhaust myself with all the effort of sleeping. Now I wake and find I haven't rolled over once or even disturbed the sheets. I'm making the most of what sleep I get, sure. But I'm not quite getting where I need to be. Because she eats every three hours, this kid.

The 9 p.m. feeding's a cakewalk—you're still awake, so you just drop what you're doing and go feed the kid. Midnight's not so bad either, because you're not yet deeply asleep when it arrives. It's all tolerable, at any rate, when compared with the soul-searching depths of 3 a.m., which finds everyone *but* you sunk in deepest dreams. What are they dreaming of, these sleeping people? Of having babies…It happens this way: After the midnight feeding you topple bodily into bed and instantly fall unconscious. About a microsecond later, you're shocked awake, responding with your entire body to the redlining, the revving, baby monitor. Impossibly, three hours have passed. You think to yourself: I cannot do it. I cannot do it. But then you get up (because the baby is crying), and you do it, and as with any responsible fright movie, the first shock is really just there to get you all worked up for the second, and the second to get you all worked up for the third. And so on. The situation finds a fresh level of complication when you wake up (because the baby is crying) at 6 a.m. to go feed the baby with the distinct impression that you already *did* the 6 a.m. feeding—at which point you realize that you were dreaming about feeding the baby in between sessions of feeding the baby. These complications achieve a Borgesian complexity when you fall asleep while feeding the baby and somehow manage to dream about feeding the baby while you're feeding the baby.*

Jessica and I are night people. Gracie, in her first weeks of life, proves to be a morning person—at eight weeks, in fact, she routinely wakes so early that she threatens to become a night person from the previous night. If she keeps moving in this direction, I can only imagine that she'll begin waking to her day at just around the time we're ready to go to bed—which, I suppose, would at least save us the effort of going to bed and having to wake up again. This means a full-service sleep overhaul, because until just a few years ago I had a job that kept me at work until long after midnight and delayed my bedtime until around the

---

* Or sometimes I wake in the dark already standing beside the bed, tearing frantically at the bedclothes, having emerged from a nightmare in which I fell asleep while feeding the baby in bed and then suffocated her by rolling over on her in my sleep. The dreams preside over my waking mood—a preschool is located five stories below our apartment. Every day, at the same hour of late morning, the students are released into the small fenced playground for recess; I often wake from troubled naps to the chaotic noise of their games, and, according to what the previous night seeded there in my heart, I sometimes think this resembles the sound of children being murdered and have to go and look to be sure this isn't what's happening.

hour I'm now being asked to wake up in the morning. The transition is a slow process, and for a long while I become a sort of sleep apprentice, a morning person in training who occasionally watches the sunrise do its thermonuclear thing over a high-rise building to the southeast (the New York City equivalent of the horizon) and thinks: All right, this isn't terrible. It's not great, but it's not terrible. I can do this. I used to watch the sun explode over a high-rise and think, I guess I'd better head off to bed now. And now I watch that same sunrise on the far side of an abbreviated night's sleep.* Unfortunately, I haven't yet mastered the ability to get to bed at a morning person's hour. I still go to bed at an evening person's hour, except I encounter a morning person's wake-up on the far side.

What's that like, living an evening person's life in the evening but a morning person's life in the morning? It's as if I'm permanently suspended in the delirium of a second straight all-nighter in college; I feel as if I have televisions for eyes, old televisions broadcasting the two-dimensional fantasy of television-land, where everything and nothing is real. Soon after I enter my sleep apprenticeship I find that I'm making mental errors at work— forgetting people's names, misplacing the name of the day of the week, spacing out on the location of weekly meetings. I cruise through my day and everything is slowed down, drowned in a syrupy languor that makes things flow along at half speed— until suddenly the blatting roar of a bus lets me know that I tried to cross the street against the light. I step back to the curb, heart racing, startled awake but already sinking back into that frowsy cloak of exhaustion. This is sleeplessness.

And then there is extreme sleeplessness. What's *that* like? Being mummified alive, I suppose. Jessica adopts a clear signal—

---

* One important thing I must note: I do these wake-ups only occasionally. Most nights, Jessica takes the wake-ups herself and allows me to sleep so that I can function at work the next day. If this is what it's like for me, I wonder, what's it like for *her*?

tears—that indicates when she's been pushed past mere sleeplessness and sent hurtling into the void. She isn't a big crier, my wife
(when offered a decision between a good cry or a bracing cup of
Barry's, she'll usually go with the tea), and when I see tears, I take
notice. The tears always arrive unannounced—I'm sitting inno-
cently beside her when, without warning, a fat droplet darkens
the crossword we're solving. I feel a flush of cold and think, OK,
my wife has been pushed too far. I think: Tonight I need to get her
to bed and take the 3 a.m. feeding myself, which means Jessica will
get maybe six hours leading up to the 6 a.m., though I'd better
get on the stick and figure out how I can get sleep myself tomorrow or I'm going to be lethally underslept.* And this is how we
become trapped in a recursive cycle of save and recover, in which
I try to help Jessica and become overextended, and then Jessica
tries to help me and becomes overextended, et cetera.

I developed a number of tricks to steal brief snatches of rest at
work during those first months, the best of them locking myself
in a conference room and sleeping through an abbreviated lunch
hour. (If I hadn't done it, I would have fallen asleep at my desk
or passed out on the subway ride home and awakened to find
myself hurtling toward Pelham Parkway long after dark.) I work
for the *New York Times* and could fairly be characterized as an
extremely focused writer—I write 363 days per year, taking off
only my wife's birthday and Christmas Day (though the truth
is that on that second day "off" I often sneak upstairs and tap
out a few paragraphs after the presents have been opened).† By

---

* Gracie was breast-fed but I was able to feed her using frozen and thawed breast
milk in a bottle.
† I don't write for the *New York Times,* though—my official title is technology editor, though it would be more informative to state that I'm a newsroom project
manager for the development of the software that the editorial staff uses to produce both the print and digital versions of the newspaper. I can't imagine working
anywhere else—this may explain why my job at the *Times* is the only nontemp job
I've held in my entire life. I came here in 1993, the same year I graduated from college, landed a job at the lowest possible newsroom position, and stuck with it. That

some strange twist of cosmic design, my desk at work is located just steps from the monumentally influential *New York Times Book Review,* and from my desk I could float a paper airplane into those neighboring desks. I suppose I would be less aware of this geographical irony if the latest novel I'm working on—my third, the book that spools away behind my sprinting cursor each morning—were working *at all.*

Writing a novel that isn't working is, I think, a lot like being drawn into an endless argument with your cleverest friend. The book always seems to have the last word, and the withering lines you *should* have parried with always come to you too late—on the evening bus home, the next morning in the shower. And what happens when you sit down at the laptop to write, all but *cracking your knuckles* in eagerness to get to it? You clam up. Or worse: You do what I do and just go on and on and on about everything, which is the same as going on about nothing at all—and the book smiles, and turns away, and knows it's beaten you. That's what it feels like, your relationship with each new book: a contentious détente, with the threat of utter collapse always hanging in the air between you. These days the work never goes where I want it to, to the point that the book seems to have about twelve heads, like a hydra or a terrible executive committee. I think I know what's going on: the paranoia seeded in the NICU has taken noxious root. The subjects that have overrun the new novel include nuclear war, the dangers of air travel, the terrors of pregnancy complications, jealousy, envy, fear, sex, alcoholism, rage, doctors, pharmaceutical addiction, and marital treachery. This is all in the first few pages of the latest work. This is all in chapter 1. Let's revisit that list of subjects: nuclear war, the dangers of air travel, the terrors of pregnancy complications, jealousy, envy, fear, sex,

---

was sixteen years ago, and not least among the reasons I've stayed is the wealth of freelance writing opportunities to be found in the building—freelance writing opportunities like the Dining In piece that was the seed of this book you're reading. But I'm getting ahead of myself.

alcoholism, rage, doctors, pharmaceutical addiction, and marital treachery. Now that's quite a list. This is the thematic list of a writer who may be having a difficult time recovering from a frightening experience. What's *happened* to me? Every word I put down seems to have been fed through a prism of suppressed panic, the thought patterns of someone who cannot digest the information coming his way quickly enough and must, like an exhausted rower beating against a current, labor and labor to merely remain in place. Move on, I think. Write something else. I do just that. I create a new, untitled document, and begin writing a new story. And what are the subjects of this new thing I try to write? Nuclear war, the dangers of air travel, the terrors of pregnancy complications, jealousy, envy, fear, sex, alcoholism, rage, doctors, pharmaceutical addiction, and marital treachery. I'm not channeling the material. The material is channeling me.

The Balkan Error, the nonworking novel in question, does have a few lighter moments. Nearly all of these occur when the main character reflects on or discusses his two-year-old daughter— who happens, coincidentally, to be named Grace. From page 36 of *The Balkan Error:*

> "I don't see retirement being a healthy thing for you, Jay. What will you do with yourself besides drink all day?"
> "I'll take Gracie to the park every afternoon."
> "And when she gets older?"
> "...She'll take *me* to the park every afternoon."

I see what I'm trying to do, here. I'm trying to project myself into a happy future, with the aid of a fictional stooge. But these future-tense daydreams are few and far between. The rest of the work reads like a dirge, an epitaph on the present. So there I am—seething on the bus, motionless under the thundering showerhead, and stuck in an endless argument with a book I can't control. Life is doing this to me, making me wish I'd said, wish

I'd said, while a terrible logic pattern plays in my head—an apparently self-renewing cycle: I won't be free of this inertia until I finish this book. But I won't finish this book until I'm free of this inertia.

In this way, the writing is both the problem and the solution.

I ask myself, as I type this, is it so surprising that the room I chose most often for those naps at work was a tiny conference room adjacent to the *Book Review?* A room where surely many an accomplished writer has made an impromptu call to his agent or editor or has paused for a moment to scribble out an idea for her next book.

What was funniest about this situation—and sad, in the way that only truly funny things are—was that the editors of the *Book Review* had begun a tradition whereby any famous writers who visited the building to give an interview or record a podcast were asked to sign this very conference room's wall. So every time I locked myself in the room to steal five minutes of rest, the last thing I would see before the narcotic haze overtook me was the inscribed signature of a literary luminary. There on the white wall I'd see the looping cursive or fiercely pointed print of Tom Wolfe, Augusten Burroughs, Richard Price, Jonathan Lethem—other names too, all carved in the author's unique hand. Because we'd moved into the building only months before I began taking these naps, there were just a few names to read. But I could only imagine that had the editors followed this tradition in the old building, and had history carried over from the old building to the new, this wall would have proclaimed the names of the true immortals: Roth, Nabokov, Stone, Trevor, Updike. What was I doing there? Attempting to sleep, yes—but also attempting to acquire some of the aura these writers had left behind. It was there, unmistakably—a benevolent haunting, a muted, ambient roar.

It's all wound together for me—the disparate, deeply pessimistic writing, the sleeplessness, the fears for my baby, my inability to find my way out of *any* of it. One hand washes the other. One morning, seething with an unidentified emotion, I seized the Magic Marker waiting there in the conference room, uncapped it, and held the point trembling to the wall. I was feeling a sort of psychic pain. I wanted my name up there, with the others. Yet I didn't even know what my next book wanted to be—I didn't have what was necessary to get my name up on the wall.

All I left behind was a single point: a period, which identifies the death of a thought.

This is sleeplessness—the marriage of all the forces I must overcome but can't: because I'm underslept. If you're a lucky new parent, mere sleeplessness is the place where you spend most of your time for those first three or four or five months. It is a place that people without children usually find themselves no more than once or twice a month—that night when you had a cold, say, and couldn't get to sleep or that time a problem at work kept you awake grinding your teeth all night. You suffered a bit the next day, but you got through it. Yet people without children almost invariably have the option, some option, for catching up the next day—for example, canceling that dinner out with a friend and instead heading home to get to bed by nine—while new parents are just staring down the loaded barrel of another night of wake-ups and feedings.

What's especially irritating about this stage is that around this time an avalanche of parenting advice—almost uniformly unwanted and certainly unsolicited—begins to flood in from family, colleagues, friends, or generally anyone on the street whom you casually tell that you have a baby. Although the people offering this advice are trying to help, the cumulative effect is to catch you at your absolute lowest and tell you that (1) this low is your fault (because you're too uptight / not uptight enough, because you're too strict / not strict enough, et cetera) and (2) if you had only handled the situation the way *they* would have, everything would be just fine. The crucial irritant is that much of this advice, even the well-meaning advice, would appear to spring from a hidden but undeniably present inner agenda—advice on how to manage a baby's sleep, for example, is usually less about helping the situation than it is about allowing the advice giver to impress his or her philosophy on sleep on the new parents, who are really just sleep-starved and overwhelmed and frightened.

Every evening, Jessica and I, sleep-deprived and overloaded with unsolicited advice, confront a renewable question: What are we to eat? When we consider the amount of time left before Gracie's next wake-up, we're tempted to answer, Bread and water. But we're already sacrificing so much. We're missing out on sleep, the common denominator that links all of life's other pleasures, and we deserve a break—so we evolve into a couple who cook with what's already in the house. See the stacked cabinet: Use what's there. Canned ingredients, dried beans, bread crumbs, spices. We use hardy staples from the refrigerator: parsley, nuts, oil-packed ingredients like anchovies, well-wrapped scallions and leeks, ageless jalapeños. And we stock up on large amounts of ingredients we'd ordinarily have to shop for day by day—bacon, knuckles of ginger, sheets of fresh pasta—and freeze them in individual servings in the freezer, where they can easily be pulled out on a whim. The message is: *Mine what you have. Let the outside world go about its business without you for a while.* We eliminate the planning, the traveling, the daily shopping, the elaborate preparation—we don't have the energy for that, and we don't need it anyway, if all we want to do is to make a decent meal. We don't need fresh bay scallops, overpriced caviar, delicate basil— instead, we make spaghetti (cabinet) with anchovies (refrigerator), walnuts (refrigerator), and bread crumbs (made with bread taken from the freezer) without leaving home. We get mileage out of white rice leftover from some Chinese takeout, combining it with scallion (refrigerator) and ginger (freezer) sauce topped with a fried egg (refrigerator). We make soups right and left—I devise a reasonable imitation of a soup my parents used to bring along on ski trips (cabinet: canned tomatoes, canned stock); Jessica wrestles an ancient container of dried lentils down from the cabinet and pairs them with carrot, leek, and celery (refrigerator), then ups the ante with white wine, crushed red pepper, and lots of thyme and bay leaf (cabinet). Soon we're eating as well as we used to, with little or no preparation.

But the success we have in the kitchen isn't being reflected elsewhere—not on the page or anywhere else. The sleep needs are and are not being met, for parents and child. We don't speak about it, but it's there, the understanding that we're taking some sort of life class—lessons taught by books, by night, and by other things—and we're *failing*. At this point, a visitor would need about five minutes in our household to establish that things have spun out of control and are about to get worse. What was a nightly horror show has come to resemble, instead, the narrative thread of a bad whodunit—and, as with any poorly executed procedural, we've spotted the villain early on. Call it what it is—reflux—and rest is the apparent victim. Reflux has come into our lives, to murder sleep.

Ginger-Scallion Rice with Fried Egg

Serves 2

Do me a favor and make this recipe even when you're not pressed for time. Something about the combination of carbs plus ginger plus scallion hits all the pleasure centers. This makes a great breakfast for two. Or lunch. Or dinner. Or snack. You get the idea.

Bunch of scallions (white and green parts), finely chopped

2 tablespoons peeled and minced fresh ginger

2 teaspoons soy sauce

½ teaspoon rice wine vinegar

5 tablespoons peanut oil

3 cups leftover rice from Chinese takeout (or
  3 cups cooked white rice)

1 egg, cracked into a bowl or ramekin, yolk intact

1. Combine the scallions, ginger, soy sauce, vinegar, and 1 tablespoon of the oil in a bowl and mix well. Allow to rest at room temperature.

2. Heat 2 tablespoons of the oil in a large skillet over high heat until shimmering. Add the rice and stir-fry until heated through, about 2 minutes. Add the scallion-ginger sauce and stir-fry an additional minute, then pour the rice onto a serving plate.

3. Place a small nonstick skillet over high heat and add the remaining 2 tablespoons of oil. When the oil shimmers, gently add the egg. When the bottom of the egg has set, gently tilt the pan and use a spoon to baste the top of the egg with the hot oil, until the yolk is partially cooked, about 30 to 60 seconds more. (Test the yolk gently with your thumb—it should be just slightly firm.) Slide the egg onto the rice and serve immediately. At the table, break the yolk with your chopsticks and stir into the rice.

Bread and Tomato Stew

Serves 2

A jacked-up version of the tomato soup I used to eat for lunch at the local rope tow when I was a kid. Most pappa al pomodoro recipes dissolve the bread into a porridgelike stew, but I prefer to set the bread apart, as toasted bread crumbs, where it contributes some crunch and contrast to the smooth tomato soup.

> 2 thick slices white bread
>
> 5 tablespoons extra virgin olive oil
>
> 2 cups canned crushed tomatoes
>
> 2 cups chicken stock
>
> ½ cup dry white wine
>
> 1 rind from a block of Parmesan cheese
>
> 2 bay leaves
>
> 2 sprigs fresh parsley
>
> 1 medium yellow onion, peeled but left whole
>
> Salt and freshly ground black pepper
>
> ½ cup freshly grated Parmesan cheese
>
> 2 pinches of chopped fresh parsley

1. Toast the bread briefly to dry it, then add the bread to a food processor or blender. Blend until crumbs the texture of coarse soil form. Heat 2 tablespoons of the oil in a large skillet over medium-high heat. When the oil shimmers, add the bread crumbs. Toast the bread crumbs, stirring and tossing frequently, until browned and nicely crisped, about 4 minutes. Pour the bread crumbs into a small bowl.

2. Combine the crushed tomatoes, stock, wine, cheese rind, bay leaves, parsley, onion, and 2 tablespoons of the oil in a medium saucepan. Season aggressively with salt and pepper. Heat over high heat to a bare simmer, then lower the heat and gently simmer, uncovered, for 30 minutes.

3. Discard the bay leaf, parsley, cheese rind, and onion. Add the grated cheese to the soup and stir to combine well. Ladle into warmed bowls, then drizzle the surfaces of the soups with the remaining tablespoon of olive oil. Top each bowl with a very generous scattering of the bread crumbs and chopped parsley and serve immediately.

Spaghetti with Anchovies, Walnuts, Mint, and Bread Crumbs

Serves 2 to 3

I've had this pasta many times, and I still think of it as an unusual pairing. Anchovies and walnuts? But the anchovies vanish into the sauce (you'll get a big hit of anchovy when they first hit the oil, but they soon fade into the background), and the walnuts lend the olive oil a wonderfully nutty undertone. But what really shines here is the homemade bread crumbs you dust the pasta with at the end. You'll see what I mean when you get that first crunchy, savory bite. And the mint brightens the whole plate.

2 thick slices white bread

½ pound dried spaghetti

6 tablespoons olive oil, plus more for drizzling

2 garlic cloves, minced

4 oil-packed anchovy fillets

¼ cup crushed walnuts

Big pinch of crushed red pepper flakes

Salt and freshly ground black pepper

½ cup dry white wine

¼ cup chopped fresh mint or parsley

Note: To crush walnuts, wrap whole walnuts in a kitchen towel and whack the towel with a pot.

1. Bring a large pot of salted water to a boil over high heat.

2. Toast the bread briefly to dry it, then add the bread to a food processor or blender. Blend until crumbs the texture of coarse soil form. Heat 2 tablespoons of the oil in a large skillet over medium-high heat. When the oil shimmers, add the bread crumbs. Toast the bread

crumbs, stirring and tossing frequently, until browned and nicely crisped, about 4 minutes. Pour the bread crumbs into a small bowl.

3. Add the spaghetti to the boiling water and cook according to the directions on the package.

4. While the spaghetti is cooking, add ¼ cup olive oil to the same skillet you used to toast the bread crumbs and place over medium-low heat. Add the garlic and anchovy and sauté, crushing the anchovies with a spoon until they fall apart, about 1 minute. Add the walnuts and sauté to toast, about 4 minutes. Add the pepper flakes. Season with salt and pepper. Add the white wine, raise the heat to medium high, and simmer for 2 minutes. By now the spaghetti should be about done.

5. When the spaghetti is done, reserve ¼ cup of the pasta water, then drain the spaghetti and add it to the skillet, along with the pasta water and the mint. Mix well, then divide onto 2 plates. Top each plate with a hefty scattering of bread crumbs (I like to use a lot, here), then drizzle with more olive oil and serve.

Black Bean Soup with Bacon and Cumin

Serves 2

If you have any corn tortillas in the refrigerator (flour tortillas won't work, so skip using those), fry sliced wedges in some hot oil until lightly browned and crisp—now you have homemade tortilla chips to go alongside the soup.

    2 tablespoons olive oil
    1 slice bacon
    1 medium onion, diced
    1 celery stalk, diced
    1 carrot, diced

½ jalapeño pepper, minced

1 teaspoon whole cumin seed

1½ tablespoons tomato paste

Salt and freshly ground black pepper

4 cups canned black beans, rinsed and drained

1 cup water

1¾ cups chicken stock

Freshly squeezed juice of ½ lime

¼ cup chopped fresh parsley, cilantro, chives, or
   scallion greens

2 tablespoons sour cream

1. Heat the oil in a medium saucepan over medium heat and add the
bacon. Cook until the bacon is browned and its fat is rendered, about
5 minutes. Remove the bacon, crumble, and set aside. Add the onion,
celery, carrot, and jalapeño and sauté until very soft, about 5 minutes,
then add the cumin seed and tomato paste. Season with salt and pepper and sauté to caramelize the tomato paste, about 3 minutes.

2. Add the beans, water, and stock. Bring to a boil, then lower the
heat and simmer for 20 minutes. Reserve 2 cups of the vegetables and
beans, then transfer the remaining soup to a blender (or use an immersion blender). Place the lid on the blender, then place a kitchen
towel over the lid to make sure hot liquid doesn't splatter. Pulse until
coarsely pureed. Return to the saucepan, add the reserved 1½ cups
beans, bring to a simmer, and add the lime juice. Serve garnished with
crumbled bacon, a scattering of parsley, and the sour cream.

DECEMBER

loneliness management

So now we're in a whodunit, a procedural, and like the talented detectives we are, we begin taking notes. The journal we keep is the only way to identify each morning what actually happened the night before. Without it we'd be asking each other, Wait, you mean you did a *second* bottle at midnight? Wasn't she sleeping after that? She spit it all up. And you did it again. How much did she eat? How long did she cry? Without a firm record to consult, the answers to these questions would be lost forever, hard nighttime truths displaced by the parallax perspective of brighter daylight. So we put it all down, every bit of relevant information: when Gracie woke up, how long she was awake, what she ate, how we were feeling at the time, what we did to resolve the situation.

It's quite a read, this bad whodunit. You can't put it down. There on the page I see unambiguous descriptors like *inconsolable* and *insane* and *shrieking* and frightening phrases like *??? can't figure it out…* and *as if in terrible pain* and *nothing worked*— and, finally, a quickly scrawled aside that brings a true shiver of empathic horror: *Do we need to see a colick* [sic] *specialist?** The

---

* Quite a few laypersons like to note, usually while pointing at the listener with a half-empty wineglass, that some pediatric specialists believe colic doesn't exist.

question hardly needs to be asked—it's the only thing on our minds all the time, though we've been avoiding addressing it. We're beginning to realize that our daughter suffers from an extraordinary case of infant reflux. Imagine the infant equivalent of crippling adult heartburn, the kind that keeps you awake all night grimacing in pain, tossing and turning, and you're close to understanding what our baby suffers after every feeding. In Gracie's case, this is an exquisitely heartbreaking form of torture, as it takes its most terrifying manifestation whenever our prematurely born and very light daughter eats well, the one thing we want her to do with every meal.

Some shrug and say, This is what babies do. They say the answer to the sleep problems is Cry It Out. Some say we should let the party in question work through her problems alone, cry it out, and learn how to fall asleep without our help.* But we're not ready to try that yet, because Jessica and I are already on Cry It Out ourselves and have been for weeks.

Well, I'm guessing these people didn't have colicky children and, anyway, it's not a good idea to make such a casual remark, because if you say it in the presence of a parent who believes his child is colicky, there is a fair chance you'll get a half glass of wine thrown in your face. The accepted logic is that a colicky baby cries a lot—but saying that a colicky baby "cries" is like saying that someone who suffers from clinical depression feels "sad." This is serious business that increases the risk of postpartum depression and can tear families apart. I don't know if Gracie was colicky or not—we know she suffered from infant reflux so severe it was indistinguishable from colicky symptoms.

* And this is the between-a-rock-and-a-hard-place aspect of our situation. Many pediatricians say that you can safely begin sleep training when the baby reaches fourteen pounds. With most babies, this happens in the first half year of life, which is important—they begin sleep training by about six months of age, which means you're establishing good sleep patterns early on. Most premature babies, however, take much longer to reach this magical number, which means they spend a much greater amount of time following undesirable sleep patterns—and this, of course, leads to lingering problems with sleep. It's just another unlucky break in the many unlucky breaks premature babies seem to get—they have to work harder for food, fight harder to catch up in their weight, fight harder to get the sleep they need—and these unlucky breaks make you want to fight all the harder on their behalf.

In the midst of all this, I experience a sudden and brief reprieve: Two days before Christmas, Jessica brings Gracie to Connecticut to begin celebrating the holidays with her family. I'll travel north by train to join them on Christmas Day, when I'm on break from the *Times*. Until then, I'll be on my own.

The wise thing for any new parent in this situation to do would be to show absolute restraint and use these forty-eight hours as a restorative break, a sort of alcohol- and stress-free spa visit without the spa. This is exactly what I don't do. Like a tempted parolee who finds that his time in stir has only whetted the taste for the illicit, I return to the scene of earlier crimes and youthful indiscretions and revert to a midtwenties frame of mind—which means that on that first night I'm shaking up my first drink before I've even taken off my coat. I follow this up by playing video games on my laptop, hacking away at my guitar, watching lousy action movies on television while reclining on the couch, and generally acting in a way that would identify me as being a useless parent and husband or at least a parent and husband who isn't doing the responsible thing during time alone. I've been looking forward to this for days, even weeks, yet the experience has a famished quality to it. I'm supposed to feel liberated, removed to a place where nothing matters and everything is allowed, but instead I find myself beset by a gloomy unease that dogs me all through the early evening.

Hours have passed before I figure it out, why I feel this way: Acute loneliness is to blame, an unwelcome companion I came to know far too well ten years ago, when I rented an apartment on New York's Upper West Side and, for the first time in my life, found myself living alone. The union of tenant and this particular home was love at first sight—it was a one-bedroom firetrap, four flights up, complete with unrenovated kitchen, mice for company, collapsing brick wall, and a nonworking fireplace

(Jessica and I learned this the hard way), but it had a private roof just twelve steps higher and, best of all, it was *mine*. I'll always remember that apartment—mostly because Jessica and I shared it for years and even held our wedding ceremony there but also because this was the place where I earned my degree in Loneliness Management.

This is a difficult degree to earn, and most of us, sadly, have one. The LM curriculum is a nightly clash with the upper limits of one's ability to tolerate solitude, and I'm sorry to report that this was a battle I often lost. Loneliness is especially pernicious in that unlike, say, a bad cold, which eventually passes, it is a constant threat. Confront a spiritually crippling Saturday night and somehow manage to get through it without beating your head against the wall, you're only going to wake up on Sunday to discover that you have another night and yet another night ahead of you, on into infinity. If you suffer too many of these nights in a row, you begin to think: Why *not* uncap the bottle of gin and keep going until it's all gone? Why *not* skip dinner and just eat dessert? Why *not* say to hell with bed and just pass out here on the couch with the television still going? Why not? I don't know why not, which may explain why I ended up doing pretty much that most nights. This is a problem you never get out in front of, loneliness, and a success one night guarantees no victory the next. Eventually the afflicted begins to lose the will to even attempt to fight back, the will to say, I will have a sensible night, watch a little television, read in bed, then click off the light before midnight. You lose the will to say this and instead begin seeking convenient forms of anesthetic relief. These are booze, food, writing, wine, the telephone, action flicks, chocolate, and other things. Anything that activates the id. Used in moderation, these things aren't harmful. But what happens when you lose the will to fight back, and the anesthetic becomes the *first* thing you reach for? When that happens, Saturday evening finds you stretched out on the floor in your boxer shorts, one hand buried in a bag of chips, the other gripping a third martini by the throat, and your head propped up on an unpublished manuscript as you watch yet another episode of *Monty Python*. This is where your night *begins*. And it goes downhill from there.

Interestingly, there are always new lows to visit. The following Saturday, for example, you may repeat the scene but this time not even bother to chill the gin.*

This was life without Jessica, and without Gracie, and it was murder. I'm never going back. No way, José. My midtwenties frame of mind: a nice place to visit, but I wouldn't want to live there. A single night in the gloomy unease of my preholiday reprieve is the most vivid reminder imaginable. It's hard work, lately, being a husband and father, but it's much harder not being a husband and father. Doing the dad thing, taking care of myself, getting to bed early, drinking less, eating right—it takes me through the old conscience car wash about once a day. I'm tired, but I somehow feel clean. Old me? Two-wheeled maximum-horsepower deathtrap on the highway, slamming my bare palm down on any taxi that got too close. New me? Sensible vehicle complete with air bag and antilock brakes. Old me? Armagnac nightcap at 4 a.m., with my liver already panting on my hip like a tired old dog. New me? Mint tea nightcap and bed by midnight. Old me? Frisbee-size bacon-egg biscuit over bucket-size sweetened coffee with cream for breakfast. New me? A slice of toast and a single espresso. The crushing responsibility of Gracie's nighttime schedule has forced me to put away all these things that were never doing me, or the loneliness, any good at all. I expected a reprieve with these two days off-duty, and I got it, but I also got a vivid reminder of just what it was these responsibilities helped me leave behind.

In this way, Gracie too is both the problem and the solution.

---

* The Russian phrase *resignation of the soul* seems to best characterize this state, which feels like a sort of spiritual surrender.

Do we need to see a colick [sic] *specialist?* That question is still very much on our minds as December winds down and January approaches. After Gracie was born, our daughter's erratic schedule asked me to become the Versatile Chef. Then sleep problems visited us, and I was forced to become the Resourceful Chef. I figured out what needed to be done, and we got by. But we're not getting by any longer, and now I'm best described as the Clueless Chef—because every piece of literature out there tells you that the first thing to do when your breast-fed baby suffers from reflux is eliminate any trace of dairy from the mother's diet. The National Digestive Diseases Information Clearinghouse, a component of the U.S. Department of Health and Human Services, notes that more than half of all babies experience reflux during the first three months of life, which suggests this is a tactic a vast number of new parents try.

And it isn't enough, getting rid of dairy, so we eliminate the second thing the literature advises you to get rid of: soy. After eliminating soy, we see modest results—now Gracie only suffers from *severe* infant reflux. (And I'm trying to show restraint here by using the word *severe* rather than the word *debilitating.* It certainly seems debilitating. Gracie suffers so badly from infant reflux that we often hear it gurgling in her throat when she tries to cry. Her voice becomes hoarse from the irritation to her esophagus. All babies spit up or occasionally overeat—our baby suffers to the point that she sometimes refuses eat, simply because she's been conditioned to associate eating with pain. This pain often manifests itself in hours-long fits of crying that test the stress limits of all parties involved. To further ease her pain, we've even begun having her sleep swaddled in her bouncy seat every night, harnessed into this upright chair that keeps her inclined and subdues the worst of the reflux with gravity.)

The cook's job in eliminating all traces of dairy and soy from someone's diet is less easy than it sounds. I'd *thought* it would be easy, of course. On the first day that we go completely soy- and dairy-free, I intentionally waltz into the grocery store after work without a plan for what I'll make that night. I can do this, I think, and I'm wrong. Half an hour after I elbow through the door I'm still walking the aisles like a lost child seeking his mama, a troubled expression on my face, pausing occasionally to pick up an item for sale, read its list of ingredients, and wince. Soy, it turns out, hides in the unlikeliest places; at this point I wouldn't be surprised to find it hiding in the flour, in the canned tomatoes, in the leafy greens in the produce aisle. Goddamn it. I am the Clueless Chef. By the end of the store visit my entire list of memorized recipes and cooking styles seems to have atomized, and all I can think of is pasta tossed with garlic and oil. The irony here is that women who breast-feed are admonished to take in a lot of extra calcium even as they're being encouraged to give up a primary source.* Trapped within the no-dairy, no-soy framework, I try Googling the phrase *list of foods high in calcium* and arm myself with enough knowledge to carry me from aisle one to the checkout counter. The next day I begin maximizing calcium-rich alternatives—dark leafy greens, salmon fillets. Almonds and sunflower seeds crowd the refrigerator drawer. I line the cabinet shelves with canned white beans. Oranges perfume the breezes passing over the windowsill.

---

* And I never lose sight of the fact that through all of this I've had the easy job. In the end, I'm just being asked to modify the way I cook—I still get to eat whatever I want, whenever I want. Jessica, on the other hand, does not. The list of foods she has had to give up during the pregnancy and after the birth includes but is not limited to coffee, tea, booze, wine, beer, rare steak, soft cheeses, rare tuna, fish with excess mercury, peanuts, smoked fish, sliced deli meats, soy, dairy, and a whole host of other esoteric restrictions that apparently threaten the health of the baby. I am facing challenges in how I cook. But I still arrive at the grocery store armed with one decisive bonus—the ability to *choose*. Which is something Jessica has less and less of.

But the needs aren't being met—we soon learn that the dietary changes we've made to Jessica's diet aren't resolving the reflux. Antacids might offer some relief, but until now we've resisted resorting to prescription medicine because the idea of medicating an infant seems extreme.

According to Jessica's journal, it's the first day of the new year when we accept that things have grown beyond our control, that something is medically wrong, and that we need to bring about a change. Actually, it's technically the *second* day of the year when we make this realization, in the early hours of January 2, which find Jessica sitting half-dressed in the rocker, crying and no longer bothering to wipe away tears, Gracie shrieking in her arms and slamming her knees repeatedly into her chest, apparently in terrible pain. I'm lying flat on my back on the wood floor in my boxer shorts with an arm thrown over my eyes, saying, "Oh my God," over and over. The episode has gone on so long and with such fury that we've all given up and are simply waiting for it to end. But it doesn't end. It goes on and on until we become genuinely frightened and begin to wonder if we need to visit the emergency room. Instead we phone our pediatrician's call service, and the extremely sleepy but extremely patient and helpful woman who calls us back recommends that we try antacid immediately. Our resistance to medication and its many unknowns, so resolute for so long, has evaporated in the face of this frightening eruption. I dress and hurry across Eightieth Street to the all-night pharmacy.

We give our jackknifing daughter that first spoonful with no small amount of interest—and watch with animal awe as within five seconds she ceases shrieking and becomes docile, relaxed, and silent.

It's as if someone has turned off an invisible switch.

For many minutes we sit there together in the dark in a trance of wonder, a family silenced, and consider what this means. We've been trying to control Gracie's reflux by controlling Jessica's diet and by adjusting Gracie's sleep position to keep her upright. That syllogism again:

Major premise: *I'm cooking for Jessica.*
Minor premise: *Gracie gets all her nourishment from Jessica.*
Conclusion: *When I cook for Jessica, I'm cooking for Gracie.*

I'm cooking for Gracie, but her reaction to the antacid makes it clear that the changes I've put in place are not enough. We need medical help.

Within days, Gracie is on Zantac, her reflux is under control, and, on the urging of our pediatrician, we begin sleep training—we begin Cry It Out, which is very well named indeed. In a nicely symmetrical touch, Cry It Out proves to be so stressful that I soon find myself on Zantac too.

Rigatoni with Rappini, Sweet Sausage, Cannellini Beans, "Rappini Water," and Mint

Serves 2 to 3

This is one of those recipes that makes me wonder, as I take the first bite, why anyone would ever want to eat a fussy six- or eight-course meal—why ever do that, when you can instead have one perfect bowl (OK, maybe two) of a pasta like this?

All the wonderful flavor aside, one bunch of broccoli rabe provides a good percentage of your day's calcium—it also provides a spectacular companion to fennel sausage, cannellini beans, and pasta. The mint added at the end is a nice bright counterpoint, as is the addition of the water you used to cook the rappini and pasta (the rappini adds serious flavor to the pasta water—try a sip after it's cooled down and you'll see). If your breast-fed baby doesn't react unpleasantly to heat and spice in your food, go ahead and add the pepper flakes to the pan along with the wine.

> Bunch of rappini (broccoli rabe), larger, tougher leaves separated from stalks and discarded, bottom inch of every stalk chopped off and discarded
>
> ½ pound dried rigatoni
>
> ¼ cup extra virgin olive oil, plus more for drizzling
>
> 12 ounces sweet Italian sausage, casings sliced off and discarded
>
> ¾ cup thinly sliced yellow or Spanish onion
>
> 2 tablespoons sliced garlic
>
> ¼ cup cubed pancetta
>
> ½ cup dry white wine
>
> ¼ teaspoon crushed red pepper flakes (optional)
>
> 1 cup chicken stock
>
> ½ cup canned cannellini beans, rinsed and drained
>
> 3 tablespoons (packed) chopped fresh mint
>
> ½ cup freshly grated Parmesan cheese (optional)

1. Bring a large pot of salted water to a boil over high heat. Chop the rappini into 2-inch lengths and set aside.

2. Add the rigatoni to the boiling water. Cook *with a timer* according to the directions on the package—when the rigatoni has exactly 4 minutes left to cook, add the rappini.

3. While the rigatoni and rappini are cooking, heat the oil in a very large skillet over medium-high heat. When the oil shimmers, crumble the sausage into the pan, and break up the largest pieces into smaller pieces with a wooden spoon. Cook, turning and stirring occasionally, until pieces are lightly browned, about 4 minutes. Add the onion, garlic, and pancetta and cook, stirring often, until softened and beginning

to darken a bit, about 3 minutes. Add the wine, and pepper flakes, if using, bring to a simmer, and reduce for 2 minutes. Add the stock and beans and simmer gently for 4 minutes. At this point the rigatoni should be ready.

4. When the rigatoni and rappini are cooked, reserve ¼ cup of the pasta water, drain the rigatoni and rappini together in a colander, then pour into the sauce. Add the reserved pasta water and the mint. Those not avoiding dairy can add the Parmesan too. Cook the pasta an additional minute in the sauce, stirring to combine well, then divide into bowls. There should be a fair amount of liquid sauce in the bottom of the pan you used to make the pasta sauce—spoon that over the pasta in the bowls. Top with a splash of olive oil and serve immediately.

Oven-Roasted Planked Salmon

Serves 2 (with a little snack left over)

Plank roasting is a process by which an ingredient is cooked on the grill and is infused with woodsmoke flavor as the board blackens. This recipe is for those who would like to try planked salmon but don't have access to a grill. Salmon has loads of healthy fats and calcium, and in my personal experience is a terrific gateway fish that leads people away from eating the same old flaky white cod over and over. Feel free to double this recipe—adjust amounts accordingly, and up the roasting time as needed. The broiling step, however, should still take the amount of time prescribed below.

I get a certain perverse pleasure out of presenting a recipe with only five ingredients.

> 1 wild-caught salmon fillet, skin on (about 1¼ pounds and
> 1½ inches thick)

1 tablespoon extra virgin olive oil

½ teaspoon salt

½ teaspoon freshly ground black pepper

1 lemon quarter for juicing

SPECIAL EQUIPMENT

Cedar plank for roasting

1. One hour before cooking, completely submerge the plank in water to soak.

2. After the plank has soaked for an hour, position a rack in the middle of the oven and preheat the oven to 350°F. Rub the entire surface of the salmon with the oil. Season both sides aggressively with the salt and pepper. Set the salmon aside on a plate to rest.

3. Lift the plank out of the water, shake dry, and place it in the heated oven, directly on the rack. Allow the plank to heat for 10 minutes, then open the oven and lay the salmon, skin side down, directly in the center of the plank. (You may want to place a second rack with a baking sheet beneath the plank to catch any drippings.) Allow the salmon to roast for approximately 20 to 30 minutes (cooking times can vary wildly, depending on the thickness of the fillet, the relative leanness of the fish, etc.), until desired doneness is almost reached. I prefer to cook the fish until almost medium-rare, with an interior temperature of 115°F the fish beginning to flake on the outside but remaining moist and opaque in the center. Overcooked salmon is bad salmon.

4. When the salmon has almost reached the desired level of doneness, turn the broiler to high and place the rack with the planked salmon a few inches beneath the broiler flame. After a few minutes the board will begin to blacken, pop, and smoke. This is exactly what you want—the surface of the salmon will also begin to darken and char in spots.

5. After about 5 minutes of broiling you should have a nicely black-

ening, smoking board, and salmon that is cooked perfectly (I find that the temperature rises about 10°F during this broiling process) and darkened nicely on top. (You should also have a terrifically fragrant kitchen.) Take the planked salmon out of the oven, allow to rest at room temperature for 3 minutes, then squeeze the lemon quarter over the fish and serve immediately, directly from the plank (leave the skin behind on the board as you serve). Add a salad on the side and you have a complete meal.

Chopped Salad with Cayenne Vinaigrette

Serves 2

Lots of calcium here, and no dairy in sight.

Any attempt to place a salad at the center of a meal calls for an arresting vinaigrette with some good acid and bite to provide backbone—hence the addition of both heat and spice to the recipe. The amounts of spice used here are just enough to wake up what's on the plate, but are subtle enough that they shouldn't give breast-fed babies any trouble.

FOR THE VINAIGRETTE

1 tablespoon white wine vinegar

1 teaspoon Dijon mustard

1 teaspoon freshly squeezed lemon juice

½ teaspoon water

1 small garlic clove, grated with a Microplane grater or mashed to a paste with a knife

Big pinch of hot paprika

Big pinch of cayenne pepper

Salt and freshly ground black pepper

¼ cup extra virgin olive oil

FOR THE CHOPPED SALAD

¾ cup quartered cremini mushrooms (from 5 or 6 mushrooms)

½ cup canned cannellini beans, rinsed and drained

½ cup cored, coarsely chopped radicchio

½ cup coarsely sliced endive

½ cup diced tomato

½ cup chopped scallions, white and green parts (from about 3 scallions)

¼ cup diced fennel (from about ½ small fennel bulb, cored, tough outer stalks peeled and discarded, wispy tops reserved)

¼ cup diced zucchini

¼ cup shredded red cabbage

4 asparagus spears, woody parts of stems discarded chopped into thin rounds

1 stalk celery, diced

1 medium carrot, diced

2 tablespoons chopped fresh parsley

2 tablespoons slivered almonds

1. *Make the vinaigrette:* Combine the vinegar, mustard, lemon juice, water, garlic, paprika, and cayenne in a glass jar or Tupperware container with a lid. Season with a pinch of salt and lots of pepper. Cover and shake. Uncover, add the oil, cover again, and shake aggressively until the vinaigrette is emulsified.

2. *Make the salad:* Combine all salad ingredients in a mixing bowl (add the wispy fennel tops too). When ready to serve, drizzle the salad with as much or as little of the vinaigrette as you like (about 4 tablespoons is right for me), mix well. Divide onto 2 plates, and serve immediately with crusty bread.

Provençal Soup with Basil Puree
Serves 4

Note the trick of blanching the basil leaves in step 1—this helps the basil puree to retain its bright green color even after it hits the hot soup. It works for pesto, too.

FOR THE BASIL PUREE

2 tablespoons salt

3 handfuls fresh basil leaves, washed

1 garlic clove

¼ cup olive oil

FOR THE SOUP

2 tablespoons salt, plus more for seasoning

2 ribs celery, chopped into ¼-inch dice

2 carrots, chopped into ¼-inch dice

1 zucchini, chopped into ¼-inch dice

½ medium fennel bulb, cored, tough outer stalks peeled and discarded, and chopped into ¼-inch dice

1 cup fresh spring peas or frozen baby peas

2 tablespoons olive oil

¼ pound pancetta, chopped into a small dice

½ large onion, chopped into ¼-inch dice

2 garlic cloves, minced

2 bay leaves

2 sprigs fresh thyme

1½ cups canned white beans, rinsed and drained

2 cups chicken stock

2 cups water

½ tomato, chopped into ¼-inch dice

Freshly ground black pepper

1. *Make the basil puree:* Bring a large saucepan of water to a boil over high heat. Add the salt, then the basil leaves. Leave the basil in the water for exactly 90 seconds, then drain in a colander or fine-mesh strainer and rinse it under cold water to stop the cooking. Squeeze excess water out of the basil. Put the basil, garlic, and oil in a blender and pulse, scraping down the sides as necessary, until basil is pureed.

2. *Make the soup:* Bring a large saucepan of water to a boil over high heat. Add 2 tablespoons of salt, then add the celery, carrots, zucchini, fennel, and peas. Boil for 3 minutes, then strain into a colander and shock with running cold water to fully stop the cooking and set the color.

3. Heat the oil in a large saucepan over medium heat. Add the pancetta and cook for 2 minutes, then add the onion and garlic and sweat until softened and transparent, about 4 more minutes. Add the bay leaves, thyme, white beans, stock, water, and tomato, and bring to a boil. Lower the heat and simmer the soup for 10 minutes to allow the flavors to mingle, then stir in the vegetables. Season with salt and pepper. Allow the soup to simmer for 1 additional minute, then discard the bay leaves and thyme. Ladle into soup bowls. At the table, just before eating, have each person stir in 1 tablespoon of the basil puree.

le cuisine silencieux

Cry It Out begins as an exercise in mitigating, or attempting to mitigate, collateral damage. The target of your campaign is *there*, in the crib, and you have a very clear idea about what you want this campaign to accomplish—but it's the innocent bystanders who seem to suffer most. The books on the subject—and there are *yards* of them—assure us that a few days into Cry It Out our child will *get it*, will figure out that sleep is something she initiates while alone in her crib, not while formed to the shoulder of Mom or Dad. The titles of these books take things a step further and assure us that not only will this transformation happen—it will happen with no outlandish crying. Within a night or two of beginning Cry It Out, though, we realize that these book titles are either lying or misinformed.* Gracie is nonplussed by our

---

* Enough with the pleasantries: I think these book titles are effectively lying. You know these books: They have titles like *Baby Sleeps with No Crying* and *Crying? No Way, Sleeping Baby* and *Sleeping Baby Didn't Cry,* and so on. These titles, unsurprisingly, reek of shrewd branding, of identikit consumer targeting, because after the title has convinced you to buy the thing, there at home with your new purchase you find, deep inside the pages, a confession that says something to the effect of, Well, yes, of *course* your baby's going to cry some, are you *totally naive*? My title is merely saying that *eventually* your baby will sleep without crying. But not at first. And don't blame me if *you,* the expectant consumer, thought that a title like *Baby*

tactical change and, rather than hewing to the Cry It Out script of drifting off within five minutes or so, gathers herself into an infant rage for an hour or more each night, sometimes close to two hours, a rage that surprises, a rage that *astonishes* with its power and force, and has the poisonous effect of turning Jessica and me against each other.

Cry It Out, then, begins as an exercise in mitigating collateral damage and soon evolves into something else: a *Pardoner's Tale*, in which the selfish desire for a glittering prize leads all participants to their doom. Fairness compels me to note that Cry It Out is really my doing. I'm the one who delivered the ultimatum that led to the switch—I had come to believe, as clearly as possible, that our previous approach of comforting Gracie back to sleep every time she awoke was making our sleep situation worse every night. Put simply, I feel responsible for this mess, the disaster of Cry It Out, and, hoping for the best, I appeal to Jessica with logic: *She has to learn to put herself to sleep at night. Until she learns to do that, she'll always have to put herself to sleep on our shoulders, and that means a lifetime of middle-of-the-night wake-ups. This is hard, but it's for the best. It makes sense, and it's going to work.* Jessica appeals back with her feelings: *I am a mother and my baby is in anguish and* you *are telling me to not go to her.* We're entirely unable to come at the problem from any perspective but our own. I think Jessica is being blind to plain sense while Jessica thinks I'm dismissing her feelings and, at the same time, being cruel to our child. Who is to blame? I'm not. Jessica isn't. During the most charged confrontations it almost seems as if nature is to blame. It almost seems as if nature wants us to be fighting and has constructed this tense situation with no intention of ever letting us out.

For months we've been comforting Gracie every time she wakes and cries, the logical, innate response, but her sleep patterns are

---

Sleeps with No Crying suggested that during this process baby would fall asleep with no crying. No, don't blame me for your misreading of the title. And thanks again for your purchase. This is why it's called Cry It Out: because even the people who claim to be helping you aren't giving you the straight truth.

self-destructing. Yet the apparent solution to the sleep mayhem—
letting her cry and learn to comfort herself to sleep—is just as
stressful. Jessica and I begin each night as a team committed to
the task ahead. But the very real stresses of listening to our child
crying unconsoled soon make themselves known. On nights when
the crying goes on for forty, fifty, sixty minutes—and this happens more often than I'd like to report and to a degree of intensity
that might have caused more tenderhearted witnesses to accuse
us of something bordering on cruelty—a mutinous mood arises
and divides the room. What are you to do when going to your
child to comfort her and not going to your child to comfort her
have the same effect? What do you do if your child *just won't stop
crying*? In the end, success—in the form of silence from Gracie's
room—is met less with a sense of triumph than it is with a sense
of unbinding relief.

The tension between us informs on one unexpected complication of parenting. While most of the challenges related to child
rearing have to do with figuring out the unknowns of your baby's
nature, the evolving identity, many of the challenges have, in a
contradictory way, nothing to do with the child. They're related
instead to the things you continue to discover about your spouse.
Most of these are minor, nuanced discoveries—attitudes about
nutrition, about how to manage difficult questions about life and
death. Some, though, are consequential discoveries in which you
realize, *I'm going to have to learn to live with this one.* It's been a
long time since I had one of these discoveries. Jessica, on the
other hand, is coming up nightly against a terrible blind spot in
my experience: babies. My position as instigator and cheerleader
of the switch to Cry It Out is sadly uninformed, and it comes
with a paltry résumé. This is, in some ways, an indication of just
how bad things have got. At this point we're a step away from a
willingness to try anything to see what sticks.

Jessica grew up in a family that was always greatly interested in
babies. Child rearing is a topic of conversation in her family in the

way cars or fishing or sports are topics of conversation in others. This alone would have been enough to give her a solid bachelor's degree in child rearing, but long before Gracie was born, Jessica topped off this theoretical degree with a genuine dual master's degree in special education and elementary education and then proceeded to lead her own classroom at a private school in Manhattan. The dual degree, and the entrained experience of running a classroom, taught her many things, though perhaps the greatest skill she reaped was a sort of moral tenacity—call it a willingness to stick by the people in her charge over the long haul, through the days when they can't seem to get *anything* right, and wait for them to live up to her expectations. Following, then, is Jessica's preparation for this child of ours: a theoretical degree, an actual dual master's degree, experience leading her own challenging classroom, truckloads of reading on the subject of child rearing. And here is the preparation I have: none. The first diaper I ever changed? Gracie's. The first baby who ever fell asleep on my shoulder? Gracie. The first baby I ever fed and bathed? Gracie.

And finding herself paired with someone with significantly less parenting knowledge than she has is just another in a chain of qualified expectations. Before we met, Jessica's expectations for the future included a suburban cape house with gabled windows, some sort of affectionate canine for a pet, a pleasantly sunlit yard, a gleaming kitchen complete with pastoral view, her own spacious suburban public school classroom, a leisurely commute by car, and relative geographical proximity to family and old friends. This was the image of a future she painted for me when we were getting to know each other. She was, she said, a woman who enjoyed the freedom and independence of life in the suburbs. But soon plans were being made for her to make the big move into the city— she was still completing her master's degree in upper Manhattan and commuting almost daily from Connecticut, and the move made sense. This woman, who had never imagined she would live in this or any other city, suddenly found that her life included not that image she'd beheld, but rather a cramped urban apartment with crumbling inset windows, unwanted mice for pets, absolutely no yard and in fact no direct sunlight all year-round, a New York City kitchen with a view of a cement wall, her own cramped urban private school classroom, a lengthy, blood-pressure-elevating commute by filthy subway car and packed bus, and relative geo-graphical distance from family and old friends.*

In other words, she gave up an idea of herself to be with me. This was where it all began—this was the first year we met. And people can take only so much, especially when the pressures of Cry It Out are added to the equation. She's coming up nightly against a blind spot in my experience, but she's also coming up nightly against an idea she'd had for herself that was never quite met and was sacrificed at least in part for a life with me. I suppose this is the subterranean fear I harbor, that she'll look in the mirror one of these days and think: This isn't the life I want to be living. And what are you to do with such a thought after you've had it?

After a number of weeks fairly crackling with spousal stress, Gracie *does* begin to get it, does begin to drift off in shorter amounts of time, with less crying, and even begins sleeping longer stretches. Cry It Out, in fact, would appear to be an unqualified success—the problem, once again, is with me. Although Gracie now goes to sleep around the same time each night, she doesn't always *stay* asleep, and these wake-ups are often my fault—because I drop a pot lid or break a glass or juggle a steel spatula while making dinner. There are, it turns out, no practical limits to the number of noises the uncoordinated cook can make in a kitchen—the sonic result of every new instance when metal meets metal, metal meets glass, metal meets marble, glass meets glass, and so on. The resulting chime invariably causes me to simultaneously wince and fume.

But I don't want to stop cooking.

---

* A New York City kitchen is defined as four tiny burners, no dishwasher, no venti-lation, and no space to move around *whatsoever.*

So I begin developing tricks that help me make dinner quietly.

I wonder about this sometimes, wonder why it is that at times when most people feel the need to cook less, I find myself cooking *more*. I've always been this way. Difficult life event in the offing? I reach for my chef's knife and get to work. Wretched day at work? All I can think of is getting home so I can crank up the oven. Bad commute? You'll find me in the kitchen cracking an egg into a pile of flour and kneading together fresh pasta. Why *is* it that I'm so drawn to the kitchen, especially at times when most people wouldn't want to be anywhere *near* one? There is the love of good food, sure, but that couldn't be it—I could, after all, just order in from one of the many spectacular delivery places in the neighborhood and be done with it. But no, I didn't do this when I lived alone, either. Instead, as often as possible, I'd use the intense focus required to cook well to distract me from the terrible loneliness that was waiting for me every evening—which, I suppose, is another way of saying that I was using cooking to care for myself. Now, as I find myself living with an accomplished spouse, I feel the need to bring as much to the family as she does, and I find myself with one skill that I earned the long and difficult way. Jessica has clearly developed her avenues for nurturing the family. It's possible that through the kitchen I'm seeking an avenue of my own. So there I am, cooking *more* at a time most people would prefer to cook less and trying to find ways to do it quietly, because this is, in some ways, the best I have to offer them.

One day, watching me go through my motions, Jessica says, "You should write about this and pitch it to Nick."* I write Nick an e-mail, sketching out Jessica's idea, and ask if he's interested. He replies, "I like it," and asks for more. At this point I'm astonished to find that I have been given the green light to write

---

* Nick Fox, the deputy editor of the *New York Times* Dining section. I had pitched him some food-writing articles previously, but none so far had made the cut. Here I feel compelled to note that the first food article I ever sold, which would later become the seed idea of this book, was essentially my wife's idea.

my first food-writing piece—eight hundred words will do, plus a recipe or two. I sit down to try to capture the nuances of this new stage on the page. I used to be the Versatile Chef. Then I was the Resourceful Chef. Then I was the Clueless Chef.

So what am I now?

I am the Silent Chef. It's 8 p.m., the hour Jessica and I would typically be shaking up evening drinks, rubbing steaks with salt and peanut oil, slapping an iron frying pan over a high flame, slinging a gratin dish under the broiler with a resounding clang, and wondering aloud whether we should watch the second half of that Hitchcock film we started the night before. A recent change to our living situation, however, prevents us from doing that. Our tiny dining room, next to the kitchen and living room, has been converted to a second bedroom. In that bedroom is a crib. And in that crib is a sleeping five-month-old.

For the first three months of Gracie's life, cooking noise wasn't a problem. During those initial months, she slept both erratically and deeply, somehow managing to doze peacefully beside a blaring television. At about four months, however, she settled into a nighttime schedule, and Jessica and I glimpsed the possibility of her sleeping for eight- or nine-hour stretches, a bounty for new parents. Unfortunately, we soon learned that in this new paradigm even the faint noise of preparing a routine meal in the next room was enough to jolt her awake, and our dinner plans would be delayed for an hour or more as we suffered through the process of listening to Gracie put herself back to sleep.

Cry It Out is tolerable exactly once a day.

The second time round it becomes Scream It Out or Shout It Out or Fight It Out.

It doesn't help that I'm a clumsy, overambitious cook. It's those moments when baby's sleep is most fragile that I always seem to flub a key move. The metal spatula, held with such confidence at breakfast, pinwheels out of my grip and clatters on the floor. I juggle the slippery aluminum pot lid. The steel pepper grinder shoots out of my hands like a bar of wet soap. An instant later I turn to see Jessica standing at the kitchen door with her arms crossed, tapping her foot, the sounds of infant grief rising from the next room. Our dinner plans are now clear: Either we'll be delaying the meal for a new round of Cry It Out, or we'll be dining with a baby in one of our laps. My wife is a patient woman, but after the fifteenth or twentieth time this happened, I think her patience started to wear thin.

How to adapt? The options were limited. I could have cooked a month ahead and lifted defrosted leftovers straight out of the microwave every night. Or we could have ordered in and paid a mint for so-so dinners prepared by others. Or we could have eaten cold cereal every night. But a whole host of factors—cost, cholesterol, poor quality—goaded me to take up my knives instead in the name of fellow space-starved New Yorkers. The challenge was to devise realistic practices for the decibel-conscious home cook.

The Silent Chef must follow a few simple yet unforgiving rules: Any busy, attention-demanding work has to happen before baby's bedtime; recipes must easily tolerate a lengthy span between prep and finish, ideally resting at room temperature to lessen the mess and effort involved in refrigerating and reheating; and the final steps, after baby's bedtime, have to be both quiet and fairly routine. The silent cook's role is analogous to that of a professional chef who slyly prepares food to a half-cooked state—steaks pre-seared to rare, risottos parboiled and then chilled—so dinners can be finished quickly, at a moment's notice, with as little work as possible. A short stint in a preheated oven or a quick visit to a hot pan are in order. Easy oven braises to finish browned meats and softened vegetables? Right on. Fresh pasta sauces half-prepared and warmed later, the pasta tonged straight from water to pan? I'm in.

Success leads to success—in the space of one week I make a

fish soup with fennel and Pernod, oven-braised chicken with garlic confit sauce, and a pasta sauce of broccoli rabe, sausage, and pecorino, all prepared early and all finished in near silence. The Silent Chef hits all his marks. Some simple changes help. I exchange metal utensils for plastic or silicone. I learn to set the table before bedtime. I avoid steaks, hamburgers, lamb chops, and other meats that tend to smoke the place up, demand a specific doneness, and overcook when reheated. I follow the professional chef's practice of mise en place, with ingredients chopped and organized before cooking begins—a practice all home cooks, not just those with children sleeping in the next room, could benefit from. I use my stove's exhaust fan as a makeshift white-noise machine to mask minor slipups. And I always, always set the pasta water over high heat at an hour that feels much too early—the clang of the pot, arresting as a dinner bell, never fails to elicit a cry from the next room and change the night's course irrevocably.

I know that moment well, from the early days of Cry It Out—the pristine silence suddenly cleaved by a single chime, the attendant wince, the rising sound of Gracie's enraged wake-up. In such moments I found solace, I found *strength*, in a most unexpected source: in a weakness otherwise known as naiveté. This is the blessing given to those who are just starting out on a new ordeal, in which they find themselves totally unaware of just how unprepared they are for the work that remains up ahead. This is how you get through the early days of Cry It Out—by being totally oblivious to what's headed your way. And naiveté carries certain benefits—a willingness to try just about *anything*, for example, to see if it will help the situation work. Learning to cook silently was just one example and, anyway, with January blurring into February, it's possible that the next stage, the next test, is already upon us. We remain, to our great fortune, entirely innocent of it and what it's bringing our way.

Fish Soup with Fennel and Pernod

Serves 2

A very forgiving recipe—you can complete the first part of the recipe hours (even days) ahead, with nothing left to do but simmer the mussels and fish for 6 to 8 minutes before serving.

1 small onion, coarsely chopped

1 stalk celery, coarsely chopped

4 garlic cloves

½ medium fennel bulb, cored, tough outer stalks peeled and discarded, and coarsely chopped, wispy tops reserved

3 tablespoons best quality extra virgin olive oil, plus more for drizzling

2 tablespoons plus 1 teaspoon Pernod or other anise-flavored liqueur

1 teaspoon crushed red pepper flakes

Salt and freshly ground black pepper

1 cup dry white wine

1 cup canned crushed tomatoes

4 whole peeled canned tomatoes, preferably San Marzano, drained and chopped

20 mussels, scrubbed and bearded (don't beard until just before cooking)

¾ pound skinless flaky white fish fillets, such as halibut, cut into 4 pieces

1. *Stage 1: Prebedtime.* Put the onion, celery, garlic, and fennel in a food processor, and pulse gently until chopped into a coarse paste.

2. Heat the oil in a large saucepan over medium-high heat. Add the coarsely processed vegetables to the pan, and sauté, stirring often, until softened, about 4 minutes. Add 2 tablespoons of the Pernod, and

boil until almost evaporated. Add the pepper flakes, and season with salt and pepper.

3. Pour in the wine, and bring to a boil. Reduce for 2 minutes, then add the crushed tomatoes and chopped tomatoes. Bring to a boil, stir, cover, and remove from heat.

4. *Stage 2: Postbedtime.* Return the saucepan to medium heat until barely simmering. Gently slide the mussels and fish into the broth. Bring the broth back to a simmer, and cook, stirring once or twice, until the mussels open and the fish is flaky and just cooked through, 6 to 8 minutes.

5. Divide the mussels and fish into warmed bowls. Pour the soup over all, and scatter with fennel tops. Sprinkle with the remaining teaspoon of Pernod (skip the Pernod if children are eating, since the alcohol is not boiled off here) and more oil. Serve immediately with crusty bread, if desired.

Farfalle with Marinated Tomatoes and Mint Oil

Serves 2 to 3

I almost feel guilty calling this a recipe—it's really just an assembly of great ingredients and clean flavors. The kick here is watching everyone eating try to figure out where all the flavor is coming from, beyond the tomatoes, olives, and arugula they see. They taste mint, they taste garlic, and they taste crushed red pepper—but they don't see those ingredients on the plate.

A few recommendations: First, don't substitute fresh pasta here, as it's more absorbent than dried and isn't recommended for recipes that use oil as their foundation. Fresh pasta is better suited to sauces that have butter as a base. Second, because delicate arugula bruises and breaks down easily, don't chop it until just before you're ready to use it. Finally—and this may seem somewhat freaky—that tomato "water" you pour off in step 3? Drink it. It's delicious. Trust me. You might even shake it with vermouth, vodka, and ice, strain it into a glass, and think of it as some sort of unholy cross between a martini and a Bloody Mary.

> 6 tablespoons best-quality extra virgin olive oil
>
> 12 large mint leaves
>
> 3 garlic cloves, coarsely chopped
>
> ¼ teaspoon crushed red pepper flakes
>
> 1½ pounds red, ripe plum tomatoes, halved, cored, seeded, then coarsely chopped (about 3 cups)
>
> ¼ teaspoon plus pinch of salt
>
> ½ pound farfalle or other dried pasta
>
> 2 large ears fresh corn, shucked, kernels shaved off and cobs discarded
>
> ½ cup pitted, coarsely chopped Gaeta, Ligurian, or Kalamata olives
>
> 1 cup coarsely chopped well-washed arugula

1. *Stage 1: Prebedtime.* Bring a large pot of salted water to boil over high heat.

2. Add the oil, mint, garlic, and pepper flakes to a small skillet. Heat over medium heat until the mint and garlic come to a light sizzle (if the mint leaves begin to pop and snap, your heat's too high; turn it down some). Stir a few times and allow to gently sizzle for 60 seconds. Turn off the heat and allow the oil to steep and cool in the pan for 20 minutes, then strain the oil and discard the solids. Set the oil aside.

3. Add the tomatoes to a large bowl and sprinkle with the salt. Toss with your hands and allow to rest at room temperature for 30 minutes. (The tomatoes will soften and throw off a bit of water.) After 30 minutes, pour off any water that's gathered beneath the tomatoes.

4. *Stage 2: Postbedtime.* Cook the farfalle according to the directions on the package. When it is almost finished cooking, add the corn kernels, olives, and arugula to the bowl of tomatoes, then add ¼ cup

of the mint oil. Toss gently with a spoon. Drain the farfalle, add to the bowl, and stir until well combined.

Divide onto plates; drizzle the remaining mint oil over and around the pasta. Serve immediately.

Roast Chicken with Shallots, Bacon, and Garlic Confit Sauce

Serves 2

I created this recipe while I was going through a weird garlic confit stage. I was roasting cloves and stirring the mashed garlic into practically everything I made, and figured, why not try that as the final step of a roast chicken recipe?

Be sure to use the chicken thighs, which are the best part of any chicken.

> 4 chicken thighs, bone in and skin on
> Salt and freshly ground black pepper
> 4 tablespoons extra virgin olive oil
> 2 tablespoons unsalted butter
> 10 shallots, peeled
> 5 garlic cloves, unpeeled
> 2 sprigs fresh thyme
> 1 slice bacon, cut into ½-inch squares
> 1 cup dry white wine
> ½ cup chicken stock

1. *Stage 1: Prebedtime.* Pat the chicken dry and season to taste with salt and pepper. Place a medium dutch oven over high heat, and add 2 tablespoons oil and 1 tablespoon butter. When the oil and butter

barely begin to smoke, lay the chicken thighs skin side down in pan. Brown well on all sides until a rich amber color, 10 to 12 minutes. Remove the chicken from the pan, and discard the fat.

2. Return the unwashed pan to medium heat, and add the 2 remaining tablespoons of oil and remaining 1 tablespoon of butter. Add the shallots, garlic, thyme, and bacon. Stir gently (so the garlic cloves don't lose their peels), until the bacon is crisp and shallots and garlic are lightly browned. Raise the heat, add the wine, and boil until reduced by half, about 3 minutes. Add the stock, bring to a boil, and season to taste with salt and pepper. Remove the pan from the heat, and set aside at room temperature.

3. *Stage 2: Postbedtime.* Preheat the oven to 350°F. Return the dutch oven to high heat. When the liquid begins to simmer, rest the chicken thighs skin side up on the vegetables. Baste quickly with stock and wine, and transfer, uncovered, to the oven. Bake 15 minutes, baste again, and bake 15 minutes more.

4. Remove the pot from the oven and transfer the garlic cloves to a small plate. Separate the cloves from their skins and discard the skins. Mash the cloves with a fork and return to the sauce, stirring to mix. To serve, discard the thyme, and place equal portions of chicken and shallots on two plates. Top with sauce. If desired, serve with rice.

Spaghettini with Black Pepper Oil, Two Peppers, and Pancetta

Serves 2 to 3

Keeping it simple here. The trick of infusing the olive oil with toasted black pepper is great for other pasta sauces too.

4 tablespoons extra virgin olive oil

1 garlic clove, finely minced

½ medium red onion, finely diced

1 teaspoon coarsely ground freshly cracked black pepper

2 ounces pancetta (or use slab bacon), finely diced

½ red bell pepper, finely diced

½ yellow bell pepper, finely diced

½ pound spaghettini or angel hair pasta

Salt

1 tablespoon minced fresh parsley

½ cup grated Parmesan cheese, plus more for garnish

½ teaspoon crushed red pepper flakes

1 tablespoon minced fresh mint

1. *Stage 1: Prebedtime.* Bring a large pot of salted water to a boil. Heat 3 tablespoons of the oil in large skillet. Add the garlic and onion and sauté for 3 minutes, until soft and transparent. Add the pepper and sauté for 2 minutes to toast the pepper and infuse the oil with the pepper flavor. Add the pancetta and sauté until just beginning to cook through, about 1 minute. Add the red and yellow bell pepper and sauté an additional minute, then turn off the heat and set skillet aside.

2. *Stage 2: Postbedtime.* Cook the spaghettini according to the directions on the box. When it has about 4 minutes to go, return the skillet with the sauce to medium heat and bring to a gentle simmer. Season with salt. When the spaghettini is ready, reserve ½ cup of the pasta water, then drain the spaghettini in a colander and pour it into the sauce. Add most of the pasta water, the parsley, cheese, and pepper flakes. Simmer for 1 additional minute, turning the spaghettini over in the sauce, to allow the flavors to mingle (if the sauce seems a little dry, go ahead and use the rest of the pasta water). Serve immediately, scattering each plate with chopped mint and additional grated cheese, and drizzling the remaining tablespoon of oil over all.

present tense

You know how it goes, because you've lived through it, and probably more times than you care to remember: the marketing push behind romance's big day. The signs of its approach begin soon after the New Year, just as the world at last seems to be quieting down and settling responsibly into its chastened Christmas hangover—you gradually become aware of a nagging exhaustion and soon realize its source: those ads breathlessly and even a little pointedly asking if you've remembered to do something special for that certain someone on Valentine's Day.* At this point, taxed television producers, even those lingering in the fringes of weather reports and cable sports channels, will rouse themselves to offer twelve-step recipes for chocolates and tips for flower arranging and to suggest questionable uses for rumored aphrodisiacs, all without any indication that they actually want to be doing any of this. Here I'm tempted to rise to my feet and ask if this isn't something we've all seen before, the equivalent of the roast turkey recipe shared by the perky talk-show host the weekend before Thanksgiving, and to ask if we can't all agree to try to do something less pro forma next year. This author would argue that the modern manifesta-

---

* Which is to say, have I remembered to spend money on her.

tion of Valentine's Day, while being marketed as an event based in sincerity of emotion, is in fact an entirely cynical enterprise that has the effect of cheapening the very thing that it claims to espouse.* And if you've already accomplished all the things that the holiday's largely unspoken but certainly implied goal is supposed to bring about—that is, if you've already *made* that baby—Valentine's Day actually presents itself as an opportunity for new parents to reflect painfully on the fact that they're doing a lot less of the lights-down-low thing than they once did, which offers a freshly ironic perspective on all the heavy breathing indeed. New parents may be doing very *little* of the lights-down-low thing, actually, and if they've had a particularly tough parenting week, this may be the *last* thing they want to do—the idea of a lengthy and luxurious shower plus eight hours of sleep probably has the greater appeal. These redirected interests lead to a little-discussed bait-and-switch of parenting: the turnabout affected by the new baby, this literalized representation of your feelings for each other, who brings a lot of love into your life while slowly causing you and your spouse to treat each other less like spouses and more like business partners—each offering the other quite a bit in the way of support and aide but very little in the way of affection and intimacy and all those other special things that married couples should give each other. There have been moments when, stymied by a child who will not be consoled, I've looked anxiously across the room and found Jessica directing a similarly questing gaze my way. We are worried by us. And an unspoken question lingers: *What have we done to us? And is the damage permanent?*

My wife is the resilient member of our union, so it's no surprise

---

* The author also reluctantly confesses that he's sometimes been found guilty of, or at any rate accused of, failing to *get in the spirit of things*—instead pursuing an analysis of the foundation and sentiments upon which various enterprises are constructed. This isn't necessarily the way he wishes to be, though the practice has certain benefits related to the writing of fiction. See John Barth's short story "Lost in the Funhouse" for a clear illustration of this compulsion and its attendant pluses and minuses.

to me when, in the early days of February, she sends me an e-mail with the subject line Meet the Sitter. It has occurred to her that the cure for this lack of intimacy is more intimacy; we will identify a sitter so that we can have a little time together away from the baby. This is no small matter—selecting the person who will act as your stand-in should the stove erupt in flames, the child swallow a penny and turn blue, the city subside to a tidal wave. *The sitter*, it turns out, is a woman who previously cared for the children of a powerful, or at any rate well-known, ex-politician, and, as a result, she has a number of juicy stories to relate about said politician. In other words, I think she's perfect for the job. But first we must pass the gauntlet of the meet-and-greet, with its pointed questions, its cautious observance of the relationship between the child and this stranger.

I come home from work early one afternoon and am introduced to a woman who reminds me of a favorite aunt. Gracie seems to like her well enough. Better yet, the sitter is an enthusiastic cook well versed in quality Italian-American recipes and before long will offer me tips on how to fry cauliflower.* Everything seems in its proper place, and Gracie allows herself to be held with a minimum of fuss. After the sitter leaves, Jessica and I turn to each other in a sort of queasy daze, and we realize what's just happened: We've just licensed ourselves to have a proper night out.

First, however, we have to deal with the cynical enterprise of Valentine's Day itself. Jessica and I have long since rejected the forced-march qualities of the holiday, and in defiance of the take-your-sweetie-out zeitgeist we give the sitter the night off and instead uphold a tradition that we've followed for six years running: Anti–Valentine's Day, in which we stay home, invite friends over, and cook Asian food. We make one concession to

---

* And I have never been a very nickname-y guy, but before long she will begin to refer to me with a nickname I sort of like, "Chef." Last thing she always asks on her way out the door: "What are we making tonight, Chef?"

our established traditions, though. With Gracie's bedroom adjacent to both the kitchen and the living room, and Gracie waking easily to unexpected sounds, noise constraints compel us to forgo the usual practice of inviting friends over to join us for dinner. It's not as if we have to tiptoe any longer—we're able to have regular conversation, listen to music, and watch movies or television whenever we want without affecting Gracie's sleep. But we've made a few timid forays into having friends over, and these evenings didn't exactly go swimmingly. Our first effort, in particular, was a disaster.

The crucial mistake that night was that I tried to make something I'd never made before. Never do this. When cooking for someone other than your significant other, never make something for the first time, because you'll invariably learn, too late, that there's something dreadfully wrong with this new recipe. In this case, Jessica's friend Kelly arrived just as I was sliding a chicken rubbed with red wine and balsamic vinegar, made according to a new recipe I'd just found, into the oven. I am absolutely, positively, dead-on certain that I followed the recipe to the letter—amounts, temperatures, everything—so I can only assume that the printer made some sort of error or that the recipe creator was working with a very different oven from mine. Whatever the reason, about halfway through the roasting of the chicken, with Gracie fast asleep, smoke suddenly burst forth from the oven and flooded the kitchen, living room, and hallway. A quick glance inside the oven revealed that the sugars in the wine and vinegar had spattered all over the walls, creating a sort of sugar crust that smoked as aggressively as a campfire—and this, of course, soon caused the smoke detector to explode to life. Within moments, our daughter was wide awake.

What followed was a serenity-atomizing flurry, beginning with an attempt to fan and fan the air beneath the smoke detector to shut the damned thing off—but the oven, now decisively jacketed in blackened red wine and balsamic vinegar glaze, was sending out new waves of smoke with each passing second, so my only choice was to open every window in the place (it was freezing outside, and soon freezing in the apartment), open the front door, turn off the oven, and pull my half-roasted chicken out. All the while, Jessica was trying to get a very, very upset Gracie back to bed while our guest did her best to appear interested in the magazine on the coffee table. And so there we were—a half-cooked chicken, a smoking, sugar-encrusted oven, a shrieking baby, an uncomfortable guest, a downcast wife, an irritated husband, all of us with an entire night ahead of us. Seized by a fresh inspiration of know-how and can-do, I grasped a bunch of damp paper towels in a pair of tongs and did my level best to scrub the oven walls, ceiling and floor, thereby eliminating the offending oven crust, then tried to get the chicken back to its roasting business. Fifteen minutes into our second attempt at roasting, the smoke began anew—and this time it was somehow stronger, thicker, more persistent. The fire alarm went off again. Gracie (who had never stopped rattling the bars of her crib, despite repeated visits to calm her) cried harder. Jessica got a look on her face I'd expect to see if someone was stabbing her with a pushpin. I realized that it was do or die: We had to finish roasting the chicken. So I opened up all the windows and the front door, let the goddamned thing smoke (by now it was about forty-five degrees Fahrenheit in the apartment), openly cursed the author of the recipe in question, and tried to put on my casual-dad veneer, without success. Kelly, too, put on her happy face. We ate, at some point.

No guests, then, for February 14. I suppose this isn't the worst thing—*no guests* is just an oblique way of stating that Jessica and I shared dinner for two on Valentine's Day, as if we were any other new couple getting to know each other. You know these couples when you pass by them, sitting there at a restaurant's outdoor table: They linger in the handsome light of infatuation, as if framed by their own private cinematographer. Holding hands, having a laugh over a glass of wine or two, doubtlessly they are thinking hard about a future with this person across the table. That's what we're thinking about too—the future—and on nights like this, with infant sleep and its attendant rituals developing a semblance of coherence and sanity, and with a dependable sitter setting us up for plenty of nights out together, it's easy to see this future in the kindest light. Nights like this help me *get it*, help me understand it's not enough to be useful to each other. We also have to care for each other, because it's all interlinked—the marriage, the family, the triangulated affections. All must be maintained with equal interest.

With the holiday safely behind us, we begin taking experimental stabs at leaving Gracie in the care of the sitter for the night. I'm more than a little embarrassed to admit that the primary emotion I feel on those first nights out is *fear*—not for Gracie but for myself and my well-being. Even weeks later, February sliding into March, as we wave down a car on the avenue and ride the taxi downtown to dinner at one of the city's temples of modernist gastronomy, I still feel as if I've misplaced a cherished talisman, and, because I've lost its charmed protection, something awful will happen to me over the course of the night—a car accident, a freak restaurant fire, an encounter with a violent mugger. The corollary logic is, *If I can just get home safe, everything will be fine.* Why is it I think I'll be safe once again after I'm home? This is supposed to be a memorable night, and I fight to get in the spirit of things. It isn't until I've resigned myself to the spectacular cocktail that opens the meal that I realize why I harbor this anxiety: a sort of Pygmalion effect, a self-fulfilling prophecy, is exerting its power. As Gracie's father I'm expected to be nothing less than courageous; therefore in her presence I'm courageous. As Gracie's father I'm expected to be unafraid; therefore in her presence I'm unafraid. But when I step outside the halo of her company, the talent for meeting that idea of myself abandons me.

This is something I'm going to have to work on.

Dinner at the temple of modernist gastronomy is overly busy, a disappointment in the extreme. It's not that it isn't good or even great. It's just that it's not the kind of thing I ever want to eat. Why do places like this always do this to me?—leave me wishing I was, instead, seated at the narrow bar at Wu Liang Ye on West Forty-Eighth Street, eating one perfect plate of the crabs with chili and ginger with my fingers. Something that was created by a chef who thinks of himself as a nurturer rather than a genius. That this chef is a genius is undisputed, but there is little soul on offer. I keep looking up from the latest course to see if someone's putting us on—everything is deconstructed, dry-iced, aerated. Each plate looks like something that ought to be displayed in a museum, and as with most museum objects, you're left with a sense that you should look but not touch. Jessica, too, is nonplussed by all the foams and soils before her, the freeze-dried trinkets. It's the culinary equivalent of a Nouvelle Vague film, when what we really wanted was a taut thriller, something that sends you back out into the night feeling reenergized. An old writing teacher of mine would have called this overwrought. That's what this is: food that's bursting with finesse and originality but utterly lacking in love and sincerity.

After dinner, taxis are hard to come by in the pissing rain, and the ride is quiet.

We're out of practice at this sort of thing.

As we pass Houston Street, Jessica, looking out her rain-dappled window, says, "That was the opposite of comfort food."

As I look out through my own streaked window, I can't help but recall another meal we had many, many years earlier and reflect on the message that memory still sends me. Totally unplanned. We were in Union Square on a broiling Sunday afternoon, humidity so thick you practically swam from place to place, the sky crying out for the relief of rain, when it occurred to us that we could drop the errands we'd planned and instead have a glass of Riesling at the bar of a very popular seafood restaurant nearby. Once inside, Jessica suggested we try to hustle a table on the outdoor deck that overlooked Sixteenth Street. It was a fifty-to-one shot in such a crowded place, but I asked—we were still getting to know each other, then, and what doesn't seem possible when you're falling in love? To our astonishment, a table outside was offered. The two glasses of wine we'd planned on instead became an entire bottle— why not? It wasn't as if we had kids to get home to—and the snack we'd considered ordering became two dozen oysters. When, much later, the first bottle turned up empty, we ordered a second. When the first tray of oysters vanished, we asked for more. It's entirely possible there was a third drink order, and even a third order of oysters. I was forking them down with horseradish and the mignonette sauce they offer alongside, adding healthy dashes of Tabasco. Everything began to run and blur at this point, though I remember that dusk had arrived by the time we picked up the check—we'd run through one shift of waiters, and the woman who'd taken over our table had sweated through her uniform.

Christ, it was hot.

Back on the avenue, we looked for a cab, and I reflected that this was one of those rare moments when life manages to meet its own promise.

I think we both felt a certain urgency to get home.

That ride was quiet too, though for very different reasons.

And Jessica somehow managed to summarize it all on *that* ride, also, looking out the opposite window with her fingers interlaced in mine: "Let's never stop being this way."

This was before the engagement, our marriage, the baby. This was where we began.

It was a very Jessica thing to say—she is the dreamy one, a believer in the higher ideals, whereas I, always the chilly pessimist, was tempted to answer that no one ever *wants* to change, not really, life just bleeds things out of you. But that would have somehow shattered the moment, so instead I knocked three times on the faux-wood veneer of the door handle, kept silent, and decided to make my own luck.

Pho Bo

Serves 2

½ pound beef tenderloin

5 cups beef stock

½ unpeeled Spanish onion

Thumb-sized knob of fresh unpeeled ginger, halved

1 star anise

½ cinnamon stick

1 whole clove

4 ounces rice noodles

Bunch of scallions (white and green parts), sliced thinly
  on the bias

¼ cup (packed) fresh cilantro leaves

Salt and freshly ground black pepper

SPECIAL EQUIPMENT

2 deep, wide soup bowls

1. Freeze the tenderloin for at least 30 minutes (this will make the beef easier to slice). Slice as thinly as possible against the grain. Lay the slices on a plate, cover with plastic wrap, and refrigerate.

2. Pour the stock into a saucepan over high heat. Bring the broth to a boil, then lower the heat to keep the stock at the barest simmer.

3. While the stock is warming, heat a dry skillet over high heat and lay the onion and ginger cut-side down on the skillet. Sear, without moving, until the onion and ginger begin to char slightly on the cut side. Add the star anise, the cinnamon, and clove to the skillet and toast for 1 minute, until fragrant, then pour the star anise, cinnamon, clove, onion, and ginger into the simmering beef stock.

4. Place the rice noodles in a large bowl and pour 1 cup of the simmering beef stock over them, then stir well. Allow the noodles to steep in the stock until soft, about 20 minutes.

5. After the noodles have steeped for 20 minutes, drain the noodles (discard steeping stock) and separate them with your fingers. Divide the noodles between 2 deep soup bowls (the high sides of the soup bowls will allow you to immerse the beef under simmering stock). Divide the scallions and cilantro between the bowls. Divide the beef slices between the bowls—you want to arrange the bowl so that the scallions, cilantro, and beef are all showing, and make sure the beef is below the raised sides of the bowl so that it can be fully immersed in stock. Season the bowls with salt and pepper.

6. When ready to serve, raise the heat to high under the broth and make sure that it's boiling vigorously. Leaving the onion, ginger, and spice solids behind in the simmering saucepan, pour a few ladles of beef stock over the noodle bowls, making the sure the beef slices are fully immersed—the hot stock will cook the paper-thin beef quickly. Serve immediately.

Kelly's Five-Onion Tofu No. 20
Serves 3

3 tablespoons Sichuan Chili Oil (page 82)

2 leeks (white parts only), cleaned well and chopped

1 small onion, diced

2 scallions (white and light green parts), chopped into ½ inch pieces

2 garlic cloves, sliced

Thumb-sized knob of fresh ginger, peeled and sliced into matchsticks (for about 1 tablespoon total of matchsticks)

1 pound tofu, drained and patted dry, cut into 1-inch cubes

3 tablespoons soy sauce

1 tablespoon sesame oil

1 teaspoon rice wine vinegar

Bunch of chives, chopped into 1-inch lengths

2 tablespoons sesame seeds

Add the chili oil to a large skillet over high heat. When the oil just begins to smoke, add the leeks, onion, and scallions and stir-fry until soft, about 2 minutes. Add the garlic and ginger and stir-fry, moving quickly, until fragrant, about 30 seconds. Add the tofu, soy sauce, sesame oil, and rice wine vinegar and stir-fry gently to avoid breaking up tofu, until well combined and the tofu is warmed through, about 1 minute. Stir in the chives; spoon onto plates, top with a scattering of sesame seeds, and serve immediately, with rice, if desired.

Kung Pao Chicken
Serves 3

Gong bao ji ding seems to be a Sichuan analog of Italian ragú—everyone does it a bit differently, but every sincere interpretation is good in its own way.

FOR THE MARINADE

1 pound boneless chicken breast, sliced into ½ inch cubes

1 tablespoon chicken stock

1 tablespoon soy sauce

1 tablespoon cornstarch

2 teaspoons Shaoxing wine or 2 teaspoons dry vermouth

¼ teaspoon salt

FOR THE SAUCE

2 tablespoons soy sauce

1 tablespoon chicken stock

1 tablespoon Chinese black vinegar or 2 teaspoons
good-quality balsamic vinegar

2 teaspoons sesame oil

2 teaspoons cornstarch

1 teaspoon Sichuan fermented chili-bean paste

1½ teaspoons sugar

FOR THE KUNG PAO ASSEMBLY

3 tablespoons Sichuan Chili Oil (page 82)

15 dried Sichuan chilies, chilies snipped in half and as many
seeds as possible shaken out and discarded (wash your hands
immediately after finishing this task)

½ teaspoon Sichuan peppercorns

2 bunches scallions, white and dark green parts separated,
both sliced into ½-inch pieces

4 garlic cloves, sliced

Thumb-sized knob of fresh ginger, sliced into matchsticks
(for about 1 tablespoon total of matchsticks)

⅔ cup peanuts

1. *Marinate the chicken:* Combine the chicken breast, stock, soy
sauce, cornstarch, wine, and salt. Mix well, then cover and refrigerate
while you assemble the rest of the dish. Take it out of the refrigerator
15 minutes before you begin to cook so the chicken isn't overly cold
when it hits the pan.

2. *Make the sauce:* Combine the soy sauce, stock, vinegar, sesame oil,
cornstarch, bean paste, and sugar in a bowl and whisk to combine. Set
aside.

3. *Assemble the kung pao:* Heat a wok or a large cast-iron skillet over
high heat until very hot, even smoking. Add the chili oil. When the first
wisp of smoke appears, add the chilies and the peppercorns. Stir-fry,

moving the chilies constantly until they're fragrant and just beginning to color, about 15 seconds. Add the chicken pieces and continue to stir constantly. When the chicken just begins to cook around the edges, after about 1 minute of stirring, add the white parts of the scallions, the garlic, and the ginger and continue to stir constantly until the chicken pieces are cooked through, 3 to 4 minutes more (slice a large piece in half to confirm that it's cooked through, with no trace of pink).

4. Add the sauce, the peanuts, and the green parts of the scallions to the pan and continue to stir and cook until the sauce becomes glossy and coats the chicken and scallions, about 1 minute. Serve immediately with brown rice.

Dan Dan Noodles

Serves 2

This recipe may seem startlingly brazen, especially to Western tastes, in its use of nearly naked chili oil as a sauce—and so it is. That's really the whole point of the thing. Neutered Americanized versions of this recipe abound, most of them featuring sketchy ingredients like creamy peanut butter and brown sugar. Resist the urge to make those recipes, and make this one instead.

In an effort to arrive at the most authentic recipe possible, I did the prudent thing—I picked up an order of dan dan noodles from the best Sichuan place in midtown Manhattan and brought the order home, where I fiddled with the ingredients and amounts until I found the combination that most closely resembled what I had in the take-out box.

FOR THE SAUCE

¼ cup Sichuan Chili Oil (page 82)

1 tablespoon soy sauce

1 teaspoon Chinese black vinegar or ½ teaspoon
balsamic vinegar

½ teaspoon Sichuan fermented chili-bean paste

½ teaspoon sesame oil

FOR THE PORK

3 tablespoons peanut oil

⅓ pound ground pork

2 tablespoons soy sauce

6 scallions (dark green parts only), chopped into 1-inch lengths

2 tablespoons Shaoxing wine or dry vermouth

FOR THE DAN DAN NOODLE ASSEMBLY

6 ounces Chinese or Japanese wheat noodles or dried
spaghetti

1. Bring a large pot of salted water to a boil.

2. *Make the sauce:* Combine the chili oil, soy sauce, vinegar, bean paste, and sesame oil and mix well. Divide between 2 medium soup bowls.

3. *Make the pork:* Heat the peanut oil in a medium skillet over high heat. When the oil just begins to smoke, add the pork and soy sauce and sauté for 3 to 4 minutes until beginning to brown. Add the scallions and sauté an additional minute. Add the wine and boil until almost completely evaporated, stirring to pick up any browned bits stuck to the bottom of the pan. Turn off the heat and set aside.

4. *Assemble the dan dan noodles:* Add the noodles to the boiling water and cook according to the directions on the package. When the noodles have about 1 minute left to cook, return the skillet with the browned pork to the heat to rewarm. When the noodles are cooked, drain well, rinse quickly under hot water, then divide between the 2 bowls with the sauce. Divide the ground pork over the top. Serve immediately and have people mix the noodles into the sauce at the table with their chopsticks.

Sichuan Chili Oil

Makes 1 cup

1 cup peanut oil

½ cup whole dried Sichuan chilies or other whole dried red chilies

¼ cup Sichuan peppercorns

Add all ingredients to a blender or food processor. Turn the machine to its highest setting and blend until the chilies and peppercorns are coarsely pureed, 20 to 30 seconds. Pour into a small skillet, using a spatula to get all the pureed chilies out of the food processor and into the oil in the skillet. Turn the heat to high under the skillet and warm the oil, stirring the pureed chilies gently, until the oil just *barely* begins to sizzle, then turn off the heat. Allow to rest off the heat for 30 minutes. Strain through a fine-mesh strainer and discard solids—the oil should have a pleasant burnt-orange color. Store oil in the refrigerator, tightly covered. (Don't worry if the oil sets up in the refrigerator— just bring to room temperature and it will return to its expected state, with no effect on taste.)

understudy

Father-daughter night is here.

I'm going to try to play this cool.

I've previously managed any number of Gracie's nighttime needs—the bath, the bottle, the tricky wake-up—but tonight the stakes are radically elevated: I'll be doing all three without assistance and with Jessica largely out of reach. She'll be at Lincoln Center, at a performance of *Tristan and Isolde*, the supposedly hexed Wagner opera, which means I could probably get hold of her with a quick text message, though the distress signal will be of limited use should things get out of hand.*

Which they won't.

Because I can do this.

No you can't. You won't be able to hack it. Tonight will just serve to underscore a suspicion we've had all along, won't it?

I can do this.

No you can't.

The night has just begun, yet I've already sunk into a divided

---

* Jessica's assessment of the night is, "I force myself to think, No news is good news. He'll call me if he really needs me." And she's leaving it at that. It is entirely sufficient, in other words, that I am present. I don't have to be good, in her mind. I just have to be *there*.

Yes-I-can-*No-you-can't* state of mind. The inner conflict literal-
izes a carefully guarded secret: that I'm in fact *intimidated* by my
wife's self-sufficiency and fear that I don't measure up.* This is
no easy thing to do: to confess your sins to yourself. In this case,
the sin is the recognition that while I'm of great use to the family with what I produce in the kitchen, I'm of questionable use
elsewhere. Taken a step further, it's possible that I've been hiding
this weak spot by masking it with an overabundance of the thing
I'm good at. Which always, conveniently, seems to unfold right
at bedtime. Can you help with the bath? *Sorry, chops are on the fire.*
Can you read her a book while I make a call? *But the peppers will
burn if I step away.* How about a bottle? *Maybe tomorrow? This
chicken is almost ready to come out.*

Sometimes I catch Jessica staring off into space with a troubled expression on her face, and I imagine that she's suffering
through a spiritually crippling inner debate just like the one
I'm having tonight—I can do this, *No you can't.* I fear, however,
that she's not wondering if she's up to the task of accounting for
our kid; I fear that she's wondering if she's up to the task of accounting for me. And what do I do, when I see that she's stuck in
this looping debate? I step into the kitchen and make something
for her—lunch, a cup of tea. Because that's what I do well, and,
true to my nature, I just keep doubling down on the thing that's
working in the hope that it will keep *on* working, and never mind
if I'm beginning to see the plan falter. Most people think that
father-daughter night is all about the dad bonding with the kid.
In my case, it's all about bonding with my wife, who I fear has
begun to worry, worry, worry about this union. I can make you a
cassoulet, sure. I can feed the urge for a *bistecca fiorentina*. But ask

---

* This is the woman, after all, who in deep midwinter fearlessly strapped Gracie
into the car and drove seven hours north to visit friends in Vermont—without
anyone else to help her through the trip. Experienced parents may scoff at this, the
challenge of taking one kid on a trip—forgetting that they were once beginners
too, unsure of their own ability to cope.

me to take care of putting the kid to bed so you can have a night off, things become far less assured.

The night isn't *all* about anxiety, of course. During the past few weeks Gracie has evolved decisively out of the newborn phase of her life—previously a passive baby who had no choice but to remain in whatever location you chose for her, lately she's become something of an amusing Houdini. Lay her on her belly on the play mat while you answer the phone, you return two minutes later to find her halfway across the rug, on her back and looking up at you with the practiced palms-up *what?* expression of a thief caught jimmying the back door of a bank. This means that you have to watch where you tread, because whenever you place her over *there*, she's invariably going to end up over *here*—underfoot, where, apparently, all the fun is.

Now she's in the kitchen doorway, on her belly on her mat, staring at an image of herself in the mirror before her. I won't lie: We have quite a bit of drool going on here—teeth could be on the way, with all their terrible trouble. I'm at the counter chopping up ingredients. *Not ordering in, Keith?* No, thanks, I'll get by just fine without help. I am, in fact, going to make something extremely difficult tonight—homemade pizza—*in addition* to putting my daughter to bed. This is what I do well, after all, and here is how you double down on the thing that's working. The success here will reflect the success there. And the success there will reflect the success here. I can do this.

No you can't.

I'll figure it out.

I'm going to enjoy this. Watching you go down in flames.

"I can do this, Gracie," I say.

She rolls onto her left side, raises her right leg like an aerobics instructor going for the burn. Kicks once, twice, grunts with effort—and then overbalances and flips onto her back. Looks up at me, arms open, palms up. *What?*

"If you can do *that*," I say, "I can do *this*."

No you can't.

My cellphone chirps. A text from Jessica—this is a thrilling sign, that *she's* the one contacting *me*. I flip open my phone and read:

Leading man hurt. Slid down a ramp. Stopped show.

"Maybe she's coming home," I say—and there is real hope in my voice, a hope that I'll be let off the hook. But that's not the point of the night, and, anyway, they have subs for unexpected events like that. The understudy, surely, is now at centerstage, in the spotlight. I identify. I chop for a while longer, and soon I'm finished with prep. Mise en place: everything in place.

Except the baby. She began over *there*. But now she's over *here*, underfoot, head half under the counter, picking up a basil leaf I've dropped and attempting to eat it. Give me that.

I carry Gracie into her bedroom, intending to give her a wipe-down with a washcloth I've dipped in warm water. Then I'll dress her in her pajamas, feed her, read her a few books, and gentle her off to sleep. The moment of victory is nearly here. If you double down, after all, the jackpot pays off twice as much. Duly legitimized as a dad who can *hack it*, I'll have some homemade pizza and drain a glass of wine in a trance of triumph, warmed by the hot afterglow of hard-earned success. I can do this.

No you can't.

What's heartbreaking about what follows is that for a while things are actually looking good. Both of us are in a good mood as I wipe her down with the warm washcloth. I'm hurrying a little bit now, zipping along—I'm late for her bedtime, a little behind after doing all that work in the kitchen—as I give her a clean diaper, dress her in a onesie and footsie, and then, while quickly bringing a towel toward her hairline to rub it dry, stab my finger into her eye.

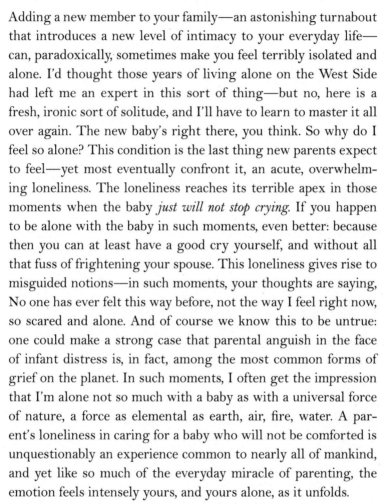

Adding a new member to your family—an astonishing turnabout that introduces a new level of intimacy to your everyday life—can, paradoxically, sometimes make you feel terribly isolated and alone. I'd thought those years of living alone on the West Side had left me an expert in this sort of thing—but no, here is a fresh, ironic sort of solitude, and I'll have to learn to master it all over again. The new baby's right there, you think. So why do I feel so alone? This condition is the last thing new parents expect to feel—yet most eventually confront it, an acute, overwhelming loneliness. The loneliness reaches its terrible apex in those moments when the baby *just will not stop crying.* If you happen to be alone with the baby in such moments, even better: because then you can at least have a good cry yourself, and without all that fuss of frightening your spouse. This loneliness gives rise to misguided notions—in such moments, your thoughts are saying, No one has ever felt this way before, not the way I feel right now, so scared and alone. And of course we know this to be untrue: one could make a strong case that parental anguish in the face of infant distress is, in fact, among the most common forms of grief on the planet. In such moments, I often get the impression that I'm alone not so much with a baby as with a universal force of nature, a force as elemental as earth, air, fire, water. A parent's loneliness in caring for a baby who will not be comforted is unquestionably an experience common to nearly all of mankind, and yet like so much of the everyday miracle of parenting, the emotion feels intensely yours, and yours alone, as it unfolds.

Stay-at-home parents (SAHPs) like my wife are especially vulnerable to the pernicious effect of this loneliness, largely because they're dealing with concentrated, drawn-out, and above all *frequent* instances of those difficult moments the rest of us only catch glimpses of now and then. And so many aspects of being a SAHP are beyond your control—for example, that babies seem to pick up a new cold about every other week, which means that plans often get altered and/or canceled at the last moment. For example, on a day in which you have plans to, say, meet your best friend from graduate school, it's not uncommon to have a phone call an hour before this meeting you've looked forward to for days or weeks or even months and hear that your friend's kid is *sick sick sick*, and, as a result, your own child shouldn't come within a mile of hers, not unless you want *your* kid to be sick sick sick. The meeting, it would seem, is off—which means that instead of bringing your child over to visit your friend and her kid, you're stuck inside with your fussy infant, staring out at the rain with the SAHP complications coming at you in vivid waves and suddenly making the whole thing seem like a bit of a raw deal. This happens about once a week. And it can really give you the blues—especially if, in Jessica's case, you're someone who cherishes her wide and deep network of friends.

Adding to the anxiety is the challenge of building and maintaining a list of friends who identify with your situation. As SAHPs go about the process of making friends with other SAHPs, they can occasionally seem (to a SAHP's somewhat amused spouse) like they're dating each other. The process of dating and picking up another SAHP are roughly the same: First, one SAHP meets another at the park or at a party or through a friend of a friend, and they discover a certain mutual attraction. They exchange phone numbers. Then they meet for a drink (though this is usually coffee or tea rather than wine). Then they go out to lunch together. Then they have the experimental dinner. Then they begin meeting up on weekends. Then they spend an entire day together. Finally, they bring their new friend around to meet the family. The lingo is the same too. Jessica will occasionally come home from a walk in the park and say, "I totally got picked up by a mother at the swings." And I will invariably respond, "Is she your type?"

Why do SAHPs do this? Pick each other up this way, and accumulate a harem of confidants? I think I know: because although having a baby unquestionably adds love, intimacy, and companionship to your life, you soon learn that there are plenty of days dispersed throughout that qualify the sweetness, days when caring for a baby can, in a very material, very confusing way, also make these things seem to go away.

Here on father-daughter night it's clear that *something's* about to leave us, though we're not quite sure what it is. Trust? Serenity? I have stabbed my kid in the eye with my finger. We both suck in a breath and are silent for an instant as we consider the gravity of this error.

Her reaction is best described as a *gathering*—of mass, of experience, of outrage. Like a professional athlete, like a shot-putter or javelin thrower striding to the line of delivery, my Gracie seems to summon her life force and place it squarely behind the primal scream that emerges. The cry is so raw that at first I fear I've injured her, lacerated a cornea, but when she wrenches around to shout even *louder* at the doorway, I get what's really happening: she's not so much telling me that she's mad about her eye, she's just telling me she's ticked that I'm the one here to comfort her afterward.

Do I try to win her back? I sing, rock, cuddle, bounce, mug, beg, coo. But I don't win her back. Efforts at offering comfort prove fruitless; to try to distract her, I get the bedtime routine going again, though she's less than happy to learn that on this evening the role of bottle giver will be played by the understudy: Dad.* Most nights Gracie drinks about two ounces of milk before bedtime; tonight she doesn't have a single drop, not one. Instead,

---

* I had given Gracie many, many solo bottles, but on those nights it was always clear that Jessica was in the next room, which allowed Gracie to nosh away with an occasional interruption—she'd suddenly wrench the bottle away and give a yell and wouldn't go back to eating until Jessica responded.

incensed, she bats the bottle away, unable to recover. It's out of my hands—we're like two terrible antagonists in this as I fight to get some milk in her, and when she begins rubbing her eyes and showing signs that she'll soon become overtired, it's clear that I have to put her in her crib and at least give sleep a try. With any luck she'll sleep an hour or two, and when Jessica gets home we'll try feeding her again. Unfortunately, luck isn't with me—I'm now paired with a baby who is exhausted yet cannot sleep, who is starved yet cannot eat, who is upset yet will not be consoled.

And this goes on for more than *five hours.** I've seen infants cry at length before—the days before we put Gracie on Zantac routinely involved hours-long stretches—but I've never, ever, seen anything like this. One would think that physical exhaustion would eventually set in and resolve the mess into a fitful slumber, but no: more than five hours. Wouldn't you run out of tears or something? Do tear ducts ever run dry? I try letting Gracie work it out on her own; I try standing in her doorway and talking sweetly; I try cuddling and bouncing; I try giving her the bottle again; I try giving her water; I try reading books; I try once again to let her work it out on her own. I try stripping her down to check that her diaper doesn't have something sharp hidden inside it, that her onesie's snaps aren't pinching her legs. I even try *showing her Jessica's picture.* Should I be embarrassed to admit that? I'm not. In the many brief intervals between all these attempts to calm her I'm in the kitchen pressing out dough, washing basil leaves, grating pecorino cheese—simple tasks that become extremely difficult to accomplish when your baby is shak-

---

* What makes this five-hour stretch especially nerve-shattering is the uncertainty factor that exists over and above the textbook stress that accompanies the sound of a crying infant—to wit, the fact that about half the time that you go to your baby to comfort her, she settles down and subsides into sleep; the other half of the time, however, visiting her merely has the effect of awaking and enraging her further. This invests every second of baby crying with a should-I-or-shouldn't-I torment of indecision. A quick cuddle may instantly resolve the problem. Or it may instantly make things worse. Your choice, Dad. And best of luck to you.

ing the bars of her crib in the adjacent room. (Having watched a few other people's babies, I've learned that while Gracie doesn't have an exceptionally high or piercing cry, hers is roughly double the volume of the crying I've heard from other kids.) Complicating my divided attention is the physiological symptom I experience every time Gracie's cries reach that frequency of vibration where sound cracks glass: sweat bursts from my every pore. It's not easy to work fresh dough with sweaty hands—the sweat-dampened flour forms a sort of pasty barrier between you and the dough and you end up looking like a guy who dipped his hands in cake batter. With so much work to do in the kitchen, I had no choice but to spend all evening in the room adjacent to Gracie's bedroom, listening to her crying, which sounds, to me, like failure literalized. It's all a blur—the kneading, dividing, flouring, rolling, shaping, seasoning, chopping, constructing, fumbling, transferring, baking, spinning, removing, resting—all of it punctuated by visits to her bedroom to try to soothe her.

I told you you couldn't do this. You may indeed help a lot in the kitchen—but I think we've firmly established that you need to work on the rest of it. And the way you work on it is with more nights like these, except they need to be nights like these in which you make something SIMPLE.

When Jessica arrives home, more than five hours later, Gracie is still crying hoarsely in the next room. I've reached that concentrated state of helplessness in which I'm simply enduring. I cannot fix the situation; I can only survive it. See me rooted to the couch with my face in my hands, my nerves worn ragged to a degree I haven't experienced since that night we gave Gracie her first dose of antacid. The night, like any responsible tragedy, could never have ended any other way, not after the way it was begun. This is where disasters are created: in the planning.

Jessica takes in the scene and seems to understand all at a glance. She approaches, places a kiss on top of my head. I think she gets it: that *I* get it, what's happened tonight. She begins stripping away the fashionable veneer that she composed before going out—off comes the fitted jacket, the opalescent pearls, the gleaming earrings. She briefly disappears into the bathroom, and when she emerges the transformation is complete—gone is the smoky eye shadow, the bee-stung lips, both swiped away by a warm washcloth—and she at last resembles the Jessica I know and love so well, the one who cautioned me, at the beginning of the night, to *maybe order dinner and focus on your daughter.*

It doesn't matter, after all, how capable you are at *anything* if those skills aren't married with discretion. Sometimes the thing you do well is the last thing the situation needs. The truth is that I need to work on helping *outside* the kitchen. When you double down and win, true, the jackpot pays off twice as much. But the corollary logic reminds us that when you double down and lose, you fall twice as hard. The smart money, as always, plays it safe.

This is experience: the lesson you learned after it was too late.

Lamb and Garlic Confit Stew

Serves 2

Best thing about this recipe, beyond ease of preparation? The 90-minute braising time—that's brief enough to allow you to make this on a weeknight after work. Walk in the door at six, you'll be eating at eight.

½ cup olive oil

1½ pounds boneless lamb shoulder, cut into 2-inch cubes

15 whole garlic cloves

4 medium leeks (white parts only), thoroughly washed and sliced into 2-inch lengths (about 3 cups total)

1 teaspoon minced fresh rosemary

2 bay leaves

2 cups chicken stock

½ bottle dry white wine

Salt and freshly ground black pepper

1. Preheat the oven to 300°F.

2. Heat half of the olive oil over high heat in a large dutch oven. When the oil just begins to smoke, add the lamb shoulder pieces and brown all over, allowing to cook mostly undisturbed, for 8 to 10 minutes total. When the lamb has about 4 minutes of browning left to go, add the garlic cloves and stir occasionally while the lamb finishes browning.

3. Move the lamb and garlic pieces to a bowl and discard any oil in the pot. Add the remaining olive oil to the pot. Return the garlic cloves to the pot. Add the leeks and sauté, stirring frequently, until soft, about 3 minutes. Add the rosemary, bay leaf, stock, wine, and season with salt and pepper. Bring to a boil and reduce for 5 minutes to concentrate the liquid. Lower the heat so the liquid is at a bare simmer, add the lamb, cover pot, and slide into the oven. Check after 15 minutes. If the sauce is boiling furiously, lower the oven temperature by 15°F. If not simmering at all, raise by 15°F. Continue checking until the sauce is just simmering. Braise for 1½ hours.

4. After the lamb is finished braising, discard the bay leaves. Serve with crusty bread to soak up braising liquid—encourage everyone eating to mash the garlic cloves in their bowl into the liquid.

Lemon Chicken Wings with Chili and Mint

Serves 2

I used to make the most complicated recipes imaginable when I was cooking for myself. Now that I know better, this is the kind of food

I make when I'm cooking for myself—a recipe so simple it practically takes care of itself, with the action taking place in a single roasting pan. I pile the finished wings on a big plate and eat them in front of the television, usually with my elbows on the table.

Don't have a roasting rack? Don't worry about it. Just lay stalks of celery in parallel rows on the baking sheet, and they'll make a perfectly fine understudy for a rack, at a cost of just pennies.

> 2½ pounds chicken wings, wingtips sliced off and discarded
> ¼ cup fresh mint leaves
> ½ teaspoon crushed red pepper flakes
> 3 cloves garlic
> Zest and juice of ½ lemon
> ½ teaspoon honey
> ½ cup whole-milk yogurt
> 1 tablespoon salt
> 1 tablespoon freshly ground black pepper

1. Place the chicken wings in a large bowl. Place the remaining ingredients in a food processor and puree. Pour puree over the chicken, combine well, then cover and refrigerate for at least 2 hours and up to 24 hours.

2. Preheat the oven to 400°F. When ready to cook, place a roasting rack on a baking sheet with raised sides (or skip the rack, and lay stalks of celery down in parallel rows)—shake any extra marinade off the chicken, then lay the chicken pieces on the rack, leaving a little space between each (use 2 baking sheets, if needed). Roast 20 minutes, remove from oven, flip pieces, and return to oven. Roast another 20 minutes, remove from oven, flip pieces, and return to oven. Roast a final 10 minutes, until wings are nicely browned. Serve immediately.

Chicken Wings with Ginger, Sesame, and Scallion

Serves 2

2½ pounds chicken wings, wing tips sliced off and discarded

2 scallions

1 jalapeño pepper (if you don't want the wings to have too much heat, slice the pepper in half and scrape away and discard the seeds)

2 cloves garlic

Half-inch knob of fresh ginger, peeled

¼ cup soy sauce

2 tablespoons sesame oil

1 tablespoon rice wine vinegar

1 tablespoon ground black pepper

1. Place the chicken wings in a large bowl. Place the remaining ingredients in a food processor and puree. Pour puree over the chicken, combine well, then cover and refrigerate for at least 2 hours and up to 24 hours.

2. Preheat the oven to 400°F. When ready to cook, place a roasting rack on a baking sheet with raised sides (or skip the rack, and lay stalks of celery down in parallel rows)—shake any extra marinade off the chicken, then lay the chicken pieces on the rack, leaving a little space between each (use 2 baking sheets, if needed). Roast 20 minutes, remove from oven, flip pieces, and return to oven. Roast another 20 minutes, remove from oven, flip pieces, and return to oven. Roast a final 10 minutes, until wings are nicely browned. Serve immediately.

Pizza Margherita

Makes two 10-inch pizzas

Have a look around the wilderness that is the online pizza-making debate—out there you will find every species of recipe, ingredient mix, and baking style known to man. The most devoted believers tend to encourage you to circumvent your oven's self-cleaning cycle, which juices the oven's ambient temperature up into the 900-degree range, and no doubt works, but places you at risk for third-degree burns, smoke in unbelievable amounts, and a visit from the fire department.

My friend, I'm here to tell you that you don't need to take that drastic step—you can get four-star results by following the steps below, which use the oven's standard functionality, and require only one piece of equipment, an iron pizza stone. (Anyway, I don't personally know anyone who's actually willing to try the self-cleaning approach.) The recipe here merely uses the stovetop (to crisp the bottom of the pizza) and the broiler (which supplies sufficient downward heat to emulate top-quality brick ovens used by the real pizza masters of New York). I eat first-quality New York brick-oven pizza at every possible opportunity, and I can promise you that the recipe below gives you comparable results at home, with no heroic measures required.

You'll note that I'm a stickler for ingredients in this one—San Marzano D.O.P. tomatoes, fresh handmade mozzarella, extra virgin olive oil. That's because this is the last place to be substituting so-so ingredients. If these specialized ingredients aren't available, I suggest you order them online or at least use the best quality you can find.

One 28-ounce can San Marzano D.O.P. whole peeled tomatoes

2 balls Pizza Dough (see page 100), given 2½ hours at room
temperature

Salt and freshly ground black pepper

2 pinches of crushed red pepper flakes

2 teaspoons extra virgin olive oil for drizzling

8 thin slices fresh handmade mozzarella cheese

12 large fresh basil leaves, washed

SPECIAL EQUIPMENT

Iron baking stone (or an iron griddle) and a pizza peel. (Please note that you must use an iron pizza stone or an iron griddle, not a regular pizza stone, for this recipe—a regular pizza stone can't take the direct flame on the stovetop. A quality iron pizza stone or griddle can be purchased online at lodgemfg.com.)

1. In the oven, position a rack so that the surface of the rack is approximately 3 inches below the broiler. Place the iron pizza stone on the rack, then preheat the broiler to its highest setting, and allow both the broiler and the pizza stone to heat for at least 15 minutes.

2. While the stone and broiler are preheating, drain the tomatoes well in a strainer. Halve the tomatoes and flick the seeds away. Transfer the tomatoes to a blender or food processor and pulse gently until thoroughly pureed. Pour into a bowl and set aside.

3. When the stone and oven have preheated for at least 15 minutes, lightly flour a work surface. Stretch 1 ball of dough to an approximate 10-inch circle—you want the dough to be thin in the middle, with a slightly raised, rounded edge for the crust. (I find that stretching yields the best crust—dimpling or pressing with the fingertips flattens the air out of the crust and makes it slightly tough.) Lightly flour a pizza peel and rub the flour over the entire surface of the peel with your hand. (You can use a flat baking sheet in place of the pizza peel.) Transfer the dough to the peel. Give the peel a shake to make sure the dough isn't sticking—if it is, gently lift the spots that stick and dust with additional flour beneath.

4. Pour about ⅓ cup of the tomato sauce into the center of the dough. Use the back of a spoon to spread the tomato sauce all around the pizza, spreading it evenly and leaving a 1-inch border with no

sauce around the edge. (Use a bit more sauce if you need it.) Season the pizza well with salt and pepper, then season with a pinch of pepper flakes. Drizzle the top of the pizza with 1 teaspoon oil.

5. Use pot holders to move the pizza stone to the stovetop. (Leave the broiler on high while you do this step.) Turn the stovetop flame under the pizza stone to the highest heat possible. (If you have an electric stove, you'll want to get the stovetop burner very hot *before* moving the stone to the stovetop, as coil burners take a lot longer to heat.) Gently slide the pizza onto the stone. Start a timer immediately— cook for about 2½ minutes, though begin checking after 2; use a flat spatula to gently lift the dough so you can peek at the underside. You're after little lines of black char here and there on the underside, with larger bits of char in some spots—it's better to slightly *overdo* it than *underdo* it. I find that about 2½ minutes is the right amount of time for this step—the pizza really won't take on much more color on the bottom after this step, so get the pizza almost where you want it to be. (The ingredients on top of the pizza will also begin to bubble, and small dough bubbles will rise up here and there.)

6. Use pot holders to slide the pizza stone back onto the rack under the broiler. Start a timer immediately again. After 90 seconds, slide the rack out and lay 4 mozzarella slices and 6 basil leaves evenly around the pizza. Spin the pizza 180 degrees. Slide the rack back in and start the timer over again. After 1½ minutes (for 3 minutes total broiling time), the pizza should be just about done. You know the pizza is done when the surrounding crust is lightly browned all around (the color of coffee with cream) with charred patches here and there.

7. Remove the pizza from the oven and serve immediately—repeat steps 3 through 6 with the second pizza. (Alternatively, you can make the first pizza and allow it to cool while you make the second—after the second pizza is made, place the pizza stone back on the stovetop over high heat, and briefly rewarm the first pizza on the stone for 30 seconds before serving both. Rewarming on the stovetop recrisps the bottom without overcooking the top.)

Grissini with Parmesan, Black Pepper, and Fennel

Makes 20 breadsticks

Grissini are rail-thin breadsticks that happen to be among the most addictive foods on the planet. Eaten before dinner with a martini, they threaten to become the whole meal.

A lot of recipes out there, however, deliver pale, pillowy, and somewhat boring results; I prefer my grissini well done, to the point that they snap in two like pencils, so I pass the sticks under the broiler before they come out of the oven.

> 2 balls fresh Pizza Dough (page 100), given 2½ hours at room temperature
>
> 2 tablespoons extra virgin olive oil
>
> ¼ cup freshly grated Parmesan cheese
>
> ½ teaspoon freshly ground black pepper
>
> ½ teaspoon kosher salt
>
> ½ teaspoon freshly ground fennel seeds

SPECIAL EQUIPMENT

Large (14 × 16-inch or more) baking sheet

Parchment paper

1. Place an oven rack in the upper third of the oven. Preheat the oven to 350°F. Cut out a square of parchment paper large enough to cover the surface of the baking sheet, and lay the parchment over the sheet.

2. Divide each of the 2 dough balls from the pizza dough recipe into 10 equal pieces, so that you have a total of 20 pieces of dough. Allow the dough to rest for 15 minutes (this will make it easier to work with).

3. One at a time, pick up a piece of dough and roll it between your facing palms, creating a long snake of dough, about the thickness of a No. 2 pencil. Each piece should be 12 to 14 inches long when fully stretched and rolled out. Lay the dough sticks on the baking sheet in parallel lines. You'll have to crowd the sticks together to fit all 20 on the baking sheet.

4. Use a pastry brush and paint the surfaces of the sticks generously with the olive oil. Sprinkle evenly with the Parmesan, pepper, salt, and fennel. Slide the baking sheet into the oven and bake for 30 minutes.

5. If your broiler is separate from your oven, slide the grissini under the broiler; if your broiler is in the top of your oven, just leave the grissini where they are. Turn the broiler to high and broil the grissini for 2 to 4 minutes, until very well browned to the color of coffee with cream. Cool on a rack or plate.

Pizza Dough

Makes enough dough for 2 medium pizza crusts or 20 grissini

An important note on measurements: Be sure to use dry-measure cups for your flour, and wet-measure cups for your water. My dry-measure cups yield a pointlessly inexact measure of water, one that throws the entire recipe off.

I've tried about a thousand combinations of all-purpose flour, bread flour, and Tipo 00 (finely-ground) flour—the pairing below gives me just the right mix of lightness, chew, and crispness that I find in my favorite brick oven places. To find Tipo 00 flour, I recommend looking online at fornobravo.com. Buy Caputo's red-bag Chef's Flour.

Note that in step 3 you're given the choice of placing the dough in the refrigerator for 2 to 3 days, or simply leaving the dough out at room temperature for 2½ hours. Leaving the dough out for 2½ hours will yield great results. Giving the dough 2 to 3 days in the refrigerator, however, will take the dough to the next level in both taste and texture. I've done side-by-side comparisons with two identical balls of dough—one given 3 days in the refrigerator, the other simply given 2½ hours at room temperature—and it was no contest. The dough allowed to age in the refrigerator was vastly superior in every way—if you have the time, I highly recommend giving the aging a chance.

> 2½ teaspoons extra virgin olive oil
> ¾ cup plus 1 tablespoon room-temperature water
> 1¼ teaspoons active dry yeast
> Good pinch of sugar
> 1 cup bread flour
> 1 cup Tipo 00 flour
> 1 teaspoon kosher salt

1. Grease 2 Tupperware containers or bowls each with a teaspoon of extra virgin olive oil.

2. Combine the water, yeast, and sugar and stir until fully dissolved. Allow to rest for a minute. Add the remaining ½ teaspoon olive oil. Combine both flours and the salt in the bowl of a food processor fitted with the dough blade. Start the machine, and add the water and yeast (again, be sure you used wet-measure cups and measuring spoons to gauge that ¾ cup plus 1 tablespoon water—accuracy is vital here) in a thin, steady stream. Process for exactly 60 seconds—the dough will come together in a ball and then whirl around the bowl as the machine kneads it.

3. Flour a work surface. Turn the dough out onto the floured surface. Divide the dough in half, and shape each half into a ball.

4. Transfer the dough balls to the two greased containers. Roll the balls around so that the entire surface is covered with olive oil. Cover the container tightly with a lid or plastic wrap and place in the refrigerator for 2 to 3 days. (If you don't want to wait that long for the

dough, you can instead leave the covered dough out on the counter at room temperature for 2½ hours—after 2½ hours at room temperature, the dough is ready to shape and bake.)

5. To prepare the refrigerated dough for baking, remove from the refrigerator, leaving the dough in its covered container, and allow to rest at room temperature for 2½ hours. The dough is now ready to shape and bake.

sweet nothings

Before me on the cutting board is a slice of Bartlett pear—or rather, what was a slice of pear before I peeled it, chopped it, and crushed it with the flat of a knife. I've been instructed to attack the thing until it's one step removed from Bartlett pear soup. I get the impression that I've done just that—it certainly looks pulverized. I set down my chef's knife and rub the back of my neck with fingers made sticky by the sugary juice.

All right. It's time.

I place a bite of the pear on a small spoon, then reconsider.

Instead, I wash my hands and place a bite of the smashed pear on the tip of my finger, turn to Gracie, and lean in.

We introduced solid foods back in March. Those early attempts were limited, though, to a few grains of oatmeal, squashed morsels of banana, quarter spoonfuls of puree of pears, all delivered with questionable success. Some of it ended up on the floor. Some of it ended up on Gracie's bib. Most of it, however, ended up on my shirt, and none of it, at any rate, ended up in her belly. The practice, in short, while being wildly fun, felt more like a lunge into a foreign environment than a deliberate stride into the real thing.

April, on the other hand, is a decisive campaign to transform mealtimes. I'm on my feet, on the move, spinning and dipping and grabbing and peeling, working away on the cutting board and enjoying the familiarity of my surroundings as I construct that rare thing: a meal that neither Jessica nor I will be eating. This meal was easy to compose, as it contained only the single ingredient of that Bartlett pear. I'm loving the change in materials, from bottles to knives, from cloths to kitchen towels. Music's playing through the laptop, Bob Marley wailing about a clown named Mr Brown who rides through town in a coffin as Gracie, locked down in her high chair, pulls on the edge of her bib and considers the action with some amusement. Until now, eating has been a process of sitting in a quiet and dark room pressed bodily against Jessica—now it's something she does in the bright, airy kitchen, while seated at a table, the wide window beside her overlooking teeming York Avenue.*

I lean in farther, a bite of pear extended. Gracie hesitates for a moment, then takes a bite.

The sensation of having Gracie take food directly from me for the first time, with no utensil or other obstacle separating me from the experience, is perhaps one of the most astonishing of my life. My first thought is, No wonder Jessica loves this. As Gracie bites away at the pear, cautiously at first, then with growing interest, finally with a dimpled smile on her face, I begin to laugh—it's an innocent laughter, childish and unselfconscious, but I soon discover that my chest has tightened, and I'm astonished to find heavy tears forcing themselves onto my lower eyelids. It's too much, all this life. I'm not just cooking for my daughter, or giving her a bottle. I'm actually feeding her. I

---

* Which explains why this is a bittersweet milestone for Jessica. This event is an indicator that our daughter is developing wonderfully, despite her challenging birth; yet it's also a reminder that Jessica will, sometime in the foreseeable future, be giving up what has been one of the most rewarding aspects of motherhood—the intimate connection she and Gracie have developed through breast-feeding.

experience this only occasionally, this sensation of being startled awake by a moment, like the sudden breath you suck in when a cold wave slaps you on the chest while wading out into the ocean. My daughter, who scared the living shit out of me by sinking into the three-pound range just days after she was born, is now eating and growing, and finally, *finally*, I'm able to contribute directly to her growth by handing her something I made expressly for her. Maybe *that's* what forced these tears to the surface—the unbinding relief of being allowed to *act*, the sense that I've finally come through the other side of this terrible Part One, a six-month stretch in which I could do little beyond watch the principal players, supply occasional support for Jessica, and hope that both my wife and child would come through intact.

I like Part Two better.

A lot.

And when did Gracie learn to feel such delight in food anyway? Until this moment, eating, the very act of it, was indivisible from the emotional aspects of bonding with Jessica. Yet her reaction to the pear suggests that she's already identified a larger truth: that food is something one enjoys emotionally, physically, and spiritually, all at the same time. I suppose it's partly the astonishingly sweet taste—I try a thick slice of the pear myself, and relish the juicy, grainy sweetness—though I'm told that breast milk has plenty of sugar to it. Sweetness can't be the source of her delight, not really. Maybe Gracie just thinks it's funny to see Dad leaning in and laughing this way, his gaze gone a little glossy and glazed, finger extended, a little bite of mashed pear on offer. I have no doubt that she enjoys every second of those quiet feedings with Jessica. But it's plain that this is a delightful experience too, which makes it a delightful experience for me. I continue as long as she shows interest, slicing off morsels of pear, chopping and smashing them with a knife, extending them to Gracie one at a time, all with my heart beating just a little too fast.

I am, I confess, ambivalent about one aspect of this switch. Eventually you've got to move past pears and bananas and oatmeal into the realm of those premade jars and packets that twin peas with carrots, pears with apples, beans with rice. Until this new stage, Gracie ate only food that came directly from Jessica—and that nourishment came indirectly from the things Jessica and I were eating. This effectively meant that Gracie's nourishment was coming exclusively from, or at any rate through, our sensibilities about what a person ought to eat and ought not to eat.* This is important, that we knew, at every step, exactly what Gracie was eating. Any conscientious person ought to, I think, pay a lot of attention to what he puts in his body. If you doubt the maxim "you are what you eat," try this modest experiment: cook two steaks—one grass fed, one grain fed—and place them side by side on a plate. Take one bite of each. You will be astonished by the difference in flavor and texture. The only real difference between the two is what type of feed was being offered, though this difference is readily apparent because *you are what you eat.* You may have a hard time conducting this test, however, because grass-fed beef can be difficult to find. Why? Grass-fed beef is more expensive to raise—so corporations rarely raise beef that way. This is, in every way, my point. Now, with the introduction of solids, the inescapable fact is that Gracie will begin eat-

---

* Ought to eat = fresh, healthy, varied plates of honestly made food whose preparation includes as few ingredients as possible, healthy fats like olive oil, and certainly no ingredients one has to struggle to pronounce, unless that ingredient is *pao hai jiao;* ought not to eat = genetically modified, chemical-soaked, bacteria-laden, poorly cooked, and cynically conceived plates of food whose preparation includes more unhealthy fats, salt, sugar, and corn syrup than one can imagine and certainly a yard or more of ingredients with names like dye number 7 and phenylacetaldehyde dimethyl acetal. The McDonald's website, for example, lists thirty-three ingredients *in the bun,* including winners like ethoxylated monoglycerides. This is why you ought not to eat McDonald's: because your lunch is more a science experiment than a meal.

ing foods made for her by corporations, which means she'll begin walking that same tightrope adults have been walking all their lives—that of finding themselves, and the foods they eat, placed at the mercy of corporate interests.

I have nothing against food made for me by others. In fact, I adore food that is made by a conscientious, talented cook—if that food happens to be Sichuan in origin, even better. But when this food is of the variety that has been conceived by a roomful of executives in suits and then prepared by a factory—packaged foods, in other words, like those that we're about to begin feeding Gracie—the question of just what it is that you're eating lurches into a hazy, undefined region that includes euphemisms like "natural flavorings" and chemicals that would preserve what's inside even if it were left unrefrigerated in the Saharan sun for a week. I have deep, deep feelings of mistrust toward these corporations. Many of them are very, very good at marketing themselves as caring, conscientious entities—but no amount of indirection can deflect the fact that their primary interest is *not* that of feeding the public quality, nourishing food. Their job, quite to the contrary, is to make money however they legally, if not ethically, can—and the stakes, judging by rising rates of obesity, heart disease, diabetes, and eating disorders, are high. These corporations are playing for money; we're playing for our very lives. Some years ago I lost a good friend from college to heart disease. *He was barely thirty years old.* There were a lot of factors involved in his death, though the poor quality of the food he was eating was certainly one of them, and one that could have been easily avoided. I reflect with amazement on all the experiences I would have missed had I died at that same age: my engagement, my wedding, marriage, the birth of a handful of nephews, my younger brother's marriage, the birth of my own daughters, the moment of first seeing one of my books in a bookstore. All would have been swept away had I suffered the same fate as this friend. I miss him. And I lament all the life he missed out on.

How did we get here? Eating poorly used to mean that you starved to death.* Now it means that you eat yourself to death. The worst of it is that I know many people—myself included—who have genuinely tried and failed to lose weight, even after adopting foods marketed as health-conscious choices. This happened to me at age thirty, soon after I realized that I was a thirty-year-old eating like a twenty-year-old. Which is to say, I was fifteen pounds overweight. In the years that followed, I tried twelve-grain health-nut oat bread, low-fat mayonnaise, decaffeinated coffee, diet soda, health bars.

None of these did a goddamn thing.

Some even caused me to gain weight.

Eventually, I realized what was happening—I was ingesting the high-fructose corn syrup, sugar, corn syrup, palm oil, chemical preservatives, and countless other counterproductive ingredients that corporations hide in these supposed "low-fat" and "diet" foods—foods that were, I repeat, aggressively marketed and packaged as being beneficial to my health.† You know these foods—the attached ads invariably feature some cool slim woman, a yoga instructor or underwear model with an imperious beauty colder and less accessible than the dark side of the moon; she's greeting the sunrise with a stretch, yawn, and grin, followed by an enraptured spoonful or bite of the food in question. Yet the reality is at odds with what's being sold. Far down the ingredient list is a string of syllables that wouldn't be out of place in a chemistry lab. High up on the list, on the other hand, we encounter some familiar villains—sugar, corn syrup, high fructose corn syrup. Why all this sweet stuff? Sweetness is a seductive flavor, and food compa-

---

* An example: the Basque people, with Franco's boot on their necks, developed a recipe for grass soup. This is eating poorly.
† One popular Italian fat-free dressing, which I routinely ate, lists high fructose corn syrup as its third ingredient, after water and vinegar. Not olive oil, not Dijon mustard. And the fourth ingredient used? *Corn syrup*—presumably to round out any flavors the HFCS failed to hit.

nies, perhaps attempting to win over consumers, may feel compelled to add more and still more sweet flavors to their products (especially those whose flavor may be compromised by fat reduction), thereby drawing consumers back through the furtive use of this oh-so-inviting taste.* High fructose corn syrup, now widely demonized, is beginning to fade from use, but look closely and you'll see that the sweetness it once supplied is being supplanted by covert substitutes like concentrated raisin juice and other such doppelgangers. This is effectively dishonest. In the end, these products are indeed "lite" in regard to their own fat content, but they're not "lite" in regard to *your* fat content.

What is the result of this yawning gulf between the advertised possibility and the cold, hard reality? You try harder; you go deeper. Into yo-yo diets. Into fad-food diets. Purges, fasts, juices. Cleanses. Now we're beginning to spin out of control. And we're *adults.* The advertised possibility is enhanced—is furthered—by celebrity magazines (often sold, conveniently, in the checkout aisles of supermarkets) supplying airbrushed images shaming you with examples of what you're *supposed* to look like. (Never mind that the people in the photographs don't look like that either—before press, every single one of those photographs has been through a gauntlet of digital enhancement, a pitiless wash cycle of autocorrect and preselect and insta-tone.) The circle is made complete when, after slyly planting a seed of self-disgust, these same sources then present themselves as the trusted friend who will talk you down from your ledge with a handy new diet.†

---

* One study I read demonstrated that rats showed a preference for sweet flavors *over cocaine.*
† Consider television shows that ask obese participants to compete in weight-loss contests. The journey will, of course, be couched in noble, life-affirming terms, which allows the broadcaster to plant itself squarely in the moral high ground, but nothing can obscure the fact that the company broadcasting this show has also, in a very contradictory way, benefited greatly by broadcasting advertisements that sell the sweetened junk that made the public overweight in the first place. So the company makes money as you gain weight; now it makes money as you lose it, too.

In other words, there is an entire *culture of trouble* out there, trouble that interlinks your health, your weight, your self-image—and my six-month-old daughter is someday going to be a sixteen-year-old woman who is concerned about her appearance, who is scrutinized and routinely taken to pieces by her peers. She will face down these same magazines in the supermarket, and with slightly less perspective at the ready. The pressures crowding in on her will, one can only imagine, be even greater than those that are exerted today. When I was a kid, you got picked on for being heavy. Now a photograph of you at the beach is forwarded to hundreds of schoolmates, with a nasty caption appended. Then you got a nasty nickname; now you end up on YouTube.

Gracie looks to Jessica and me for her cues. This has me thinking that the best way for me to raise a daughter with a healthy body image, a woman who enjoys a positive relationship with food—*a relationship that reflects, throughout her life, that sense of delight I saw in her expression when she first tasted that smashed pear*—who eats healthfully and well and does so because she respects her body and not because she hates it, is for me to have a healthy body image myself. I will not yo-yo diet. I will not purge, fast, cleanse. Instead I will try to help her maintain that sense of uncomplicated delight she felt with that taste of pear. The best way to do this, the logic suggests, is to maintain that sense of delight myself—and the best way to do *that*, as far as I can tell, is to view every shred of corporate advertising coming my way through a prism of deep suspicion and even outright hostility. The fact is that there are very powerful and crafty forces out there who want only to feed us sweet tempting nothings—not just food but also images that plant troubling notions about oneself—so that, unsatisfied, famished, and nettled, we'll return for more.

Someday, surely, compelled by the sinister effects of marketing and peer pressure, my daughter will crave fast food. I know I did when I was younger. I suppose I'll have to let her go ahead and eat it and decide for herself. As with so many aspects of parent-ing, the more I tell, advise, instruct, and lecture, the less she's going to listen and learn. Instead, when she tells me she's walk-ing out the door to go meet a friend for a sit-down of fast food, I'll pick up the nearest pear, turn to her, take a bite, and tell her to have fun.

Maybe that image will follow her out the door.

I have, in the end, a decisive advantage over those corpora-tions. They want only Gracie's money. I, on the other hand, hap-pen to love her deeply and want nothing but her happiness and well-being. I'd like to believe that with a little patience and time, my interests will win out.

buon appetito, bambino

In every relationship there comes a moment when you first betray the other person. If you're lucky, this is also the last time you betray the other person—afterward you sit around the house with your face in your hands, penitent and utterly alone, promising yourself you'll never do such an awful thing again.

Whenever Gracie needs help now, any sort of help with a doll or a book or a toy, I go to her, and she responds by swiftly making it clear that she doesn't want Dad's help. Who does she want? Mom. If I try to brush this off and help her with the doll or book or toy, finesse the moment by asserting agency as her father, she dissolves into enraged tears, shoves me away, and reaches toward her mother; and the instant Jessica touches her, Gracie becomes placid and happy again and grins with mother-love through the still-fresh tears weighting her lower eyelids. Our five-hour opera should have prepared me for this, but I'm somehow totally unready for the emotions tied up in this development, the sense of *rejection* that seethes through the simple act.* The first time this

---

* And I confess that this plays to a fear I've harbored since Jessica and I first talked about having a baby: "What happens," I asked her, "if the kid just *doesn't like me?*"

happens I'm so shattered that I allow Jessica to take over, then stand alone in our darkened bedroom for ten minutes to collect myself. I've been spurned by one of the most important women in my life, and somehow I'm unable to employ the plain sense I so badly need. Kids do this sort of thing, right? Don't they? This is a completely normal turn of events, but the emotions involved cloud my perspective. I know what's going on here. The cause of this widening divide between father and daughter is a logic series that will sound familiar to many working parents, one that renews itself into eternity. It goes something like this:

I'm away all day, five days a week,
earning the paycheck
that pays the rent
that houses the family
that includes the daughter who does not connect with me because

I'm away all day, five days a week,
earning the paycheck
that pays the rent
that houses the family...

And so on. This logic is doubly problematic because not only is it self-renewing—it also exerts a sinister power over your most selfish instincts.

Example: Whenever I carry Gracie in the shower (it's easier than the bath, and quicker, and more fun, besides) she always responds to that first thundering rush by clinging desperately to my neck. The sensory input is just too overwhelming. There is real fear in that grip—a fear that telegraphs father-love and father-need. She clings to me as long as I keep her under that first rush of the showerhead, usually a second or two, and then I take her back out and she relaxes.

The night after Gracie first rejects me, I take her in the shower and hold her under the stream. She clings to me with real fear, with genuine father-love and father-need.

And I don't take her out.

We stay there under the noisy rush. She clings to me, and I let it go on as long as I can bear, my face burning with shame and relief.

One afternoon in early May, Jessica lures me into a hardware store near our apartment, saying she wants to show me a gadget she's thinking of buying. We pace the aisles until we arrive before a compact food mill. I'm an obsessive collector of kitchen tools, but when I lay eyes on the thing I'm skeptical. Composed of three white plastic pieces—a base, a basket, and a hand crank—the food mill is too small, almost a toy, and will never stand up to the rigors of, say, grinding its way through a bushel basket of tomatoes. And this is a dangerous habit to get into—that of collecting stuff you really don't need. You already have an apartment stuffed to the rafters with baby books and baby clothes and baby toys and baby furniture and baby wipes and baby diapers, to the point that it often seems as if a very tiny, messy, acquisitive, and above all *jobless* college friend has moved in with you, along with all of her schwag. I tell Jessica that I think we should hold out for something a little more robust, and Jessica waits patiently until I get it: The mill isn't for me. It's for Gracie.

We walk out armed with our new mill, and before the day is done Jessica has shoved those premade jars of food into the back of the cabinet and has begun instead to make her own meals for Gracie; no chopping, pounding, or pulverizing required. There are, it turns out, no limits to the foods that can be easily and expeditiously put through a food mill. Zucchini, squash, sweet potato, pasta, beans, peas, pears, apples—the menu is a vegan's dream. Do my eyes deceive me, or can I actually *see* my daughter growing healthier, happier, with each day that passes? When I glance aside at her, she seems to glow with a halo of vigor; but then so does Jessica, exultant in her success. Though I'm merely a spectator in this, I find a curious satisfaction in the fact that Jessica's managed to set aside those premade foods I mistrust. This is my wife: corporation thwarter, preservative slayer, additive assassin.

And then it gets better.

A few days later, she calls me at work.

Jessica: You're going to love this.
Keith: Tell me.

Jessica: Ask me what Gracie had for lunch.
Keith: What did Gracie have for lunch?

Jessica: Gracie had pasta for lunch.
Keith: Which she's had before.

Jessica: The pasta *we* had for dinner last night. *Your* pasta.

It takes me a moment to figure out what she's telling me: that I cooked my first meal for my daughter last night. And I didn't even know it.

When I was a kid, one of the benefits of your birthday was that you were allowed to pick what the family would have for dinner. *What would you like to have?* my parents would ask, and beginning around the age of twelve my answers converged around one unifying, utterly predictable, assertion: *I want the lemon chicken man to make dinner.*

The lemon chicken man was, of course, my dad. A serious Cantonese fan from way back (the man likes his roast pork), he'd discovered an article in a magazine—a cursory search in Google

Books reveals that the magazine was volume 103 of *Esquire*—in which the writer, who identified himself as the lemon chicken man, dismissed the starchy Chinese takeout lemon chicken many of us know as a sham; he then presented a recipe so that the ambitious home cook might make the genuine article himself. My father soon made it, and oh, man, it was *good*—so astonishingly good that I immediately said, "I want to have this for my birthday." I said the same thing the following year. And I said the same thing the year after that, and the year after *that*, on into high school. The page my father had torn from the magazine soon became admirably bespattered with peanut oil, dried question marks of slurry of corn starch and water, and even the occasional lemon seed—then it vanished, though this was no tragedy, as my father had made the recipe so many times he no longer needed to refer to the article and could compose the dish from memory. I've never much liked my birthday—something about the way Father Time swivels and leers in your direction makes me feel heart-stoppingly mortal—but I remember feeling deeply happy—*safe*, really, that's a better characterization of what I felt—as I watched my father compose that lemon chicken recipe. I remember the process so vividly—the corn starch batter, the quick flash fry, the sautéed scallions, the sauce of chicken stock and fresh lemon juice and even fresh lemon slices, all of it handsomely poured out onto a platter—that I, too, could probably make it without that recipe. I'm sure I wouldn't like it half as much as I once did, though, because the aspect I enjoyed most about the process was the moment of sitting down to have a meal that someone had made expressly for me.* Even as a kid, I used to think, I'd like to do this for them someday. It's no surprise

---

* And these meals always ended with a customized birthday cake my mother had made for me, too, usually an image of whatever was important in my life at the time—as often as not, a baseball glove. My mother is famous for her cakes. How famous? One family friend actually *asked her to make his wedding cake.* She was delighted to help out and even frosted the thing in the parking lot just before heading into the reception.

to me that I cook for my parents almost every time I see them now; they made me understand how good it feels.

Cooking for Gracie makes me feel less helpless, less at the mercy of invisible forces, less talentless, but it also helps me raise my gaze optimistically to a potential new stage on the horizon, one that I hope will involve less cooking for Gracie, and much, much more cooking *with* Gracie. And is it possible that there is a stage beyond that—so far off in the future as to seem like nothing more than a shimmering mirage? A stage in which I'm not cooking for Gracie any longer but she's, instead, cooking for me.

These things pay forward. It's time to begin cooking for three.

To be safe, I consult two pediatric nutrition specialists. Dr. Jatinder Bhatia, a member of the committee on nutrition for the American Academy of Pediatrics, likes the meal-sharing idea. He says feeding a child a range of foods encourages the child to be more adventurous at the table as she moves into her second year. "This is how you teach your baby to develop likes similar to yours," he says. "Otherwise, how would an Indian child eat curry or a Mexican child consume salsa?"* Dr. Bhatia does have some concerns about introducing a wide range of foods, including allergic reactions. Many experts warn against giving babies egg whites, shellfish, nuts, citrus fruits, beans, and wheat before they are a year old, though Dr. Bhatia says some data on which those warnings were based have been refuted. Still, he says, new foods should be started carefully. "When a parent introduces new foods, he should wait five to seven days before introducing another," he says. "Just so you know the child is tolerating the food." He says, however, that it isn't necessary to wait until every minor ingredient of a recipe—herbs or spices, for example— have been tried by your baby. Also, he says, salt should be sharply

---

* And it's not just the palate that's being developed. Subtle changes are informed, I think, by what happens in the kitchen, at the table—it's been my experience that people who are adventurous with what's on their plates are adventurous elsewhere in life too.

limited if adults plan to share their meal with a baby, although a small amount can be added during preparation—for example, when salting pasta water.

The most important issue, Dr. Bhatia says, is for parents to be aware of choking hazards and to avoid foods and textures that present a risk. While puréed foods are good for babies age six to ten months, Amy Gates, a pediatric nutritionist who works with Dr. Bhatia, says that chewable foods, which are generally introduced between ten and twelve months, should be cooked until they can be squashed easily with a fork, and bites should never be larger than a large raisin. "Any food placed in the child's mouth should be able to be swallowed as is," she says, "no chewing required."

With these rules in mind, Jessica and I begin expanding the repertory of what we feed Gracie, and we're surprised by the flavors that interest her. Ravioli with sage butter, Pecorino, and crispy sage leaves? Sure, if we add some water to smooth out the pasta, which becomes gummy after it visits the food mill. Lentils milled with caramelized onions and wilted arugula vanish in a few bites. Sole Milanese leftovers give us a dynamite first effort with flaking up simple white fish. We can't keep pesto in stock, finding it a welcome complement to almost any vegetable, meat, or bean. Adding a little bit of light, sweet fruit, like pureed or mashed pears, rescues a number of attempts that might have otherwise been clunkers. Meats that have little fat, like turkey or chicken, are a bit too dry after they've been milled, and always need some added moisture. We have better luck milling up cooked-through steaks and lamb chops, although when Gracie begins eating bite-size pieces we learn that well-done steaks and chops are just too tough, so we switch to tender braised meats like short ribs, carefully chopped against the grain. To help her get some of the omega-3 fatty acids nutritionists strongly recommend, we stir in olive oil and flax oil.

A few weeks later I have dinner at the kitchen table with Gracie, my chin propped up on my fist as she examines the plate before her. This dinner is a little peace offering for my smash-grab affection-stealing gambit of holding her under the showerhead. I'm sorry, I'm sorry. She's eating braised cannellini beans mashed up from our dinner last night. I had hoped for this, the father-daughter meal and, with as much optimism as I could manage, I made an extra serving last night. I figured, She prefers her mother's company lately, but you have to keep trying. I watch as Gracie dips a finger in the smashed beans, has a taste. Likes it. Then picks up a second piece, studies it for a moment, and holds it out to me so that I can have some.

What *is it* with these stupid tears, suddenly just *there* on my lower eyelids?

Is it that some moments are too intimate, too vivid to process?

Or is it that now, just a month after I've begun feeding her—when I find myself most in need of it—she's begun feeding me?

Sole Milanese with Poached Vegetables and Chive Oil

Serves 2 adults and 1 baby at least 10 months old

Sole manages to be lighter yet more interesting than typical chicken Milanese. And the sole's extreme flakiness makes it perfect for repurposing for a child.

> Bunch of chives, coarsely chopped
>
> 2 garlic cloves
>
> ¾ cup extra virgin olive oil

1 teaspoon whole black peppercorns

1 bay leaf

2 large egg yolks

¼ cup all-purpose flour

¼ cup cornmeal

¼ cup panko or other bread crumbs

¼ cup finely grated Parmesan or pecorino cheese

1 pound gray sole fillets

6 fingerling potatoes, halved lengthwise

2 medium carrots, peeled, diagonally sliced ½-inch thick
(about 1½ cups)

2 small zucchini, diagonally sliced ½-inch thick

2 tablespoons (¼ stick) unsalted butter

Salt and freshly ground black pepper

Note: Limit the salt you use until after the child's portion has been set aside. Before serving, make sure baby has tried fish and the vegetables and has had no allergic reaction. Never leave a child eating solid foods unattended.

1. *For adults:* In a blender or food processor, puree the chives, 1 garlic clove, and ½ cup of the oil. Set aside for at least 1 hour or overnight. Strain and discard the solids, reserving the oil.

2. Bring a large saucepan of water to a boil, and add the peppercorns, bay leaf, and remaining garlic clove. Place the egg yolks on a large plate and stir with a fork. On another large plate, combine the flour, cornmeal, panko, and Parmesan. Dredge the sole in the egg, then the flour mixture until well coated. Set aside.

3. Add the potatoes to the boiling water. Four minutes later, add the carrots. One minute later, add the zucchini. When the potatoes are tender, drain and rinse well with very cold water. Discard the peppercorns, garlic, and bay leaf.

4. Place a very large skillet over medium-high heat, add the remaining ¼ cup of oil and the butter. When the butter foam subsides, gently slide in the fillets and fry, without moving, until golden brown, about 3 minutes. Flip and brown for 3 more minutes. Place the fillets in the center of two plates, setting aside a portion for baby; keep warm.

5. Mix the vegetables with a few tablespoons of the chive oil. Set aside a portion for baby, divide the rest over the fillets for adults, and drizzle the chive oil around each plate. Season adults' food with salt and pepper.

6. *For baby:* Peel the reserved zucchini and potatoes; discard skins. Puree the vegetables in a food mill or food processor. Mash and flake the fish with a fork, making certain fish pieces are pea-sized or smaller, very soft, and free of bones.

7. Stir the fish pieces together with vegetables and moisten, if desired, with olive oil, water, milk, or formula. Before serving, take a bite to be sure it is soft enough.

Bruschetta with Cannellini Beans, Rosemary Oil, and Pan-Roasted Sweet Garlic

Serves 2 adults and 1 baby at least 10 months old

6 thick slices sourdough or other artisanal bread

6 tablespoons extra virgin olive oil, plus more for drizzling at the table

2 sprigs fresh rosemary

7 garlic cloves

½ cup diced yellow or Spanish onion

¼ cup dry white wine

1¾ cups canned cannellini beans, rinsed and drained

1 tablespoon (packed) chopped fresh parsley

Salt and freshly ground black pepper

Note: Limit the salt you use until after the child's portion has been set aside. Before serving make sure baby has tried all ingredients and has had no allergic reaction. Never leave a child eating solid foods unattended.

1. *For adults:* Preheat the broiler. Toast 2 of the bread slices briefly to dry them, then add them to a food processor or blender. Blend until crumbs the texture of coarse soil form. Heat 2 tablespoons of the oil in a large skillet over medium-high heat. When the oil shimmers, add the bread crumbs. Toast the bread crumbs, stirring and tossing frequently, until browned and nicely crisped, about 4 minutes. Pour the bread crumbs into a small bowl.

2. Wipe out the skillet and allow to cool for a few minutes. Add 3 tablespoons of the oil and the rosemary to the skillet and place over medium-high heat. Bring the rosemary to a light sizzle, simmer gently for 60 seconds, then turn off the heat and allow to steep for 10 minutes. Discard the rosemary and return the skillet to medium-high heat. Add 6 of the garlic cloves and sauté, stirring occasionally, until the cloves are beginning to lightly brown, about 4 minutes. Add the onion and sauté until it takes on some color and softens, about 4 minutes. Add the wine and simmer until almost completely evaporated, about 4 minutes. At this point the garlic cloves should be fairly soft— use the back of a wooden spoon to gently mash them into the sauce. Add the beans and parsley, season with salt and pepper, and heat the beans through, stirring gently to combine, for about 2 minutes. Pour into a serving dish.

3. Toast the remaining 4 bread slices under the broiler. Rub the bread slices with the remaining garlic clove and drizzle with the remaining tablespoon of oil. Serve alongside the beans and the bowl of

crisp bread crumbs while the toast is still warm. At the table, spoon the beans onto the toast, top with a good dusting of bread crumbs, then drizzle with additional olive oil and eat.

4. *For baby:* Pass beans through a food mill or mash with a fork. Add a tablespoon or more water to bring beans to desired consistency and warm slightly in the microwave before serving. Take a bite before serving to confirm that the temperature isn't too hot.

there will be blood

In June, while we're on vacation in New Hampshire, a week in a lakeside cabin without air-conditioning, Mother Nature does the thing we least want her to do—she decides not only to turn on her heater, but to turn it to *high*. There on our first sweltering afternoon, shadows cowering at our feet, one question is on everyone's lips: How high will she go? Very high, provided your definition of *very* includes triple-digit temperatures. When night sweeps in at last, the lake turns the equation upside down with temperature inversions—stand on the front deck listening at the darkness long enough, eventually the horizon will flicker and God will crack his bullwhip. This low-pressure system is no mere meteorological fling; it decides to stick around for a while and get comfortable.

On the third night, as we're readying Gracie for bed, I casually glance at the Weather Channel and see a temperature of 90 degrees Fahrenheit displayed. This is at eight o'clock at night, and there isn't a wisp of breeze to speak of. Jessica and I bring every fan in the house into Gracie's room and open all three of her windows as wide as they'll go—but the fan blades are just beating away at tropical air, shoving it around to little or no gain. Gracie doesn't want to go down quietly in such a warm space, and I sympathize—just sitting in there with her, going through her bedtime routine, has me looking like I've just lost two sets of tennis. After about an hour of finessing the situation with sips of water, extra layers of clothing removed, and fans aimed so their swirling air passes directly over her crib, an alarming transformation takes place: Gracie, ordinarily a dynamo of infant motion, becomes pale and hollow-eyed and uncharacteristically lifeless—we take her out of her crib and begin to wipe her body down with rags soaked in cold water. Gracie's eyes flutter and her body relaxes into our arms, as if to say, *OK, thanks. Thanks for finally getting it. Maybe next time I won't have to make such a scene or bring myself to the edge of heat exhaustion.*

It's ten o'clock before we feel she's sufficiently hydrated, and the air temperature has dropped to a tolerable eighty degrees. This heat has to end. Soon Shalagh will visit with the girls, and we'll be managing *three* children in hundred-degree-plus weather.* More problematically, I'll be cooking for a group—a hazard, in my case, that introduces a possibility, however faint, of a visit to the emergency room.

I need to master cooking for a group. I'm a pro at cooking for one. I'm not bad at all at cooking for two. I'm even fairly good at cooking for three. At four, though, the social order of the kitchen begins to slew toward trouble—and when we lead into five, six, seven, and beyond, things rapidly move beyond mere disorder into open anarchy. When I cook for ten I devolve into the sort of cook who is parodied in laugh-track sitcoms, with smoke rising from the broiler, a horror-flick stripe of red sauce bisecting the wall, a garnet-saturated Band-Aid affixed to my thumb, and the

---

* Shalagh Blanck who, along with her husband, Geoff, first introduced Jessica and me. The girls are daughters Emma and Annecy.

fire department knocking at the door in full gear. It doesn't stop there: At various points in my cooking history I've prepared dinner for twelve, for fifteen—once for eighteen. If ten transforms me into a parody of a bad cook, you can imagine what eighteen did for me. You would think at some point I'd have mastered this act of putting food on the table for others, but no, my history of cooking for others remains checkered at best for a wide range of reasons—the first time Jessica and I invited her cousin over for dinner, for example, I nearly had to cancel at the last moment owing to injury.* Jessica learned about this potential cancelation when she received, at work, a text message from me that said something to the effect of

We maz hv 2 cancl dimneq

Whatever it was I wrote, she replied, quite understandably, *What?*

I'm sure my second effort at explaining myself wasn't any clearer—by then my phone and its keypad were slippery with blood, I was in a great deal of pain, and I was simultaneously searching the white pages (now the red-smeared white pages) for the address of the nearest hospital, where, I hoped, someone would be able to sew back on the tip of my index finger, which I'd nearly sliced off. I cut myself badly while making dinner for Jessica's cousin because I'd made a mistake I often make: With guests coming over for dinner, I felt the need to impress and therefore tried to make, at the last moment possible, a recipe that had many, many complicated steps and that I'd never made before.† So what happened? I fell behind—because things always take longer than

---

* Here the reader will recall this book's February chapter, with its account of my attempt to roast a chicken for a guest.
† In the case of the nearly amputated index fingertip, corn soup with lobster salad and chili oil.

you expect, especially the first time—and I tried to make up the difference by chopping my prep at lightning speed. Well, over-exertion, wandering attention, bad luck, and the sharp edge of my chef's knife soon put a stop to that, and within moments I was sending Jessica the fated text message and leaving red hand-prints on every white surface of our apartment.

I don't always cut myself before a dinner party, of course. Some-times I cut myself during the party. And I find that the evening's mood sours a bit when I creep past our guests saying, "No, no, it's nothing, just a scratch," while describing a garnet trail from the cutting board to the bathroom, where the blood-smeared Band-Aid box awaits. I tell them it's just a scratch, but it never is. It's always something worse, followed by a lengthy period of chastened recovery. And it turns out that it's exquisitely difficult to change diapers, give baths, read books, or even pick up your kid when you have a deep and painful gash on one of your fin-gertips. Before long your *daughter* is all streaked with blood, to the point that *she* looks like she had an accident, which provides a healthy shock for your dinner guests indeed.

My left hand does the knifework; my victimized right hand suffers its partner's misadventures. At last count the right had no fewer than eleven scars, which ignores the fact that many of my scars have scars, and that some of *those* scars have scars; some of my scars, in fact, are scars from where other scars were lopped off. Certain recipes virtually guarantee a good bleeding. The Vegas odds on homemade salsa, for example, would be even at best—after chopping tomatoes for five minutes my hands get all slippery, and then bad luck and wandering attention do the rest. The Cuisinart blade (fantastically, satanically sharp) carries a whole host of dangers in its edge. I use the Cuisinart to puree soups, so if it's *minestra* night, you can bet your last buck that I'll have the kitchen looking like a Jackson Pollock painting before cleanup is through. And avocados seem to have it out for me; a coldhearted kitchen observer who had watched me injure myself numerous times while slicing avocados once referred to my guacamole recipe as *sangre de cocina.**

Even Gracie gets it, has figured out that something's not quite right here. Now, for example: see the questing look she's directing toward my bandaged hand as I compose a simple breakfast—the eggs, the bacon. She's sitting in a Shaker high chair that's been used by three generations of our family, which invests her gaze with a weighty sense of being interviewed by history.

She points to my hand. (= *What's that?*)†

I say, "A Band-Aid."

She points again. (= *Why is it there?*)

I say, "I cut myself."

That ought to be the end of it, our little question-and-answer session, but her eyes, probing and relentless, continue the conversation.‡ The point-and-respond questions, you see, never end. Just yesterday, while we were on the dock, Gracie pointed at the sky (= *What is that?*). "That's the sun." Then she pointed at the sky again (= *What's it doing there?*). "It's keeping us warm." Then

---

* It probably didn't help that he was always trying to talk to me while I was making it. I have, you see, a terrible Achilles' heel: I find it difficult to hold even the simplest conversation while making a recipe I don't have completely memorized—the gray matter required to follow directions would appear, at least in my case, to be the same gray matter required to hold an A-to-B dialogue. I don't want to be impolite, so I muddle through as best I can. Which is unwise, because time has taught me that doing both at the same time virtually guarantees *there will be blood*.

† The point-and-answer questions will, fairly soon, evolve into her first attempts at using words, two in particular: *Ih?*, which is a catchall interrogative, and *Eh,* which is a catchall declarative. Soon after, *Ih?* will evolve into the infinitely more recognizable *Whaddat?*

‡ And here a scowling critic somewhere rises to his feet and derisively asks, "Do they? Do her eyes really continue to ask questions? Do they entreat, beseech, inquire? No, no, let me guess: as in a bad romance novel, they *implore,* don't they?" Reader: my daughter can ask questions with her eyes and that is a *fact*. The effect is that of a camera's unblinking gaze, and as with a camera, you get the impression that all answers are being *recorded*.

she pointed at the sky again (= *Why is it warm?*). "Because..."
et cetera, on into eternity.

She points again. (= *Why did you do that?*)

I say, "Because I was doing too many things at once."

And then I end the conversation. Because if I keep it up I'm
going to do what I always do when trying to cook and hold a
conversation at the same time: I'm going to cut myself.

And I've got only one kid. What if I have two someday, or
three? They're going to want to talk, after all. My parents, God
help them, had *four*—which meant they were effectively *always*
cooking for a group. Every day, every meal—my mother did fifteen of them, minimum, per week, and yet I can't remember ever
seeing her cut herself. My father, too. I think that's because by
the time I had got old enough to form memories of the kitchen,
they had figured things out, had realized how to get things done
with a minimum of chaos.

Theirs was a two-tiered strategy. The first tactic was to physically exhaust us every day by whatever means available—more
often than not by having us do more laps than I care to remember in the local YMCA pool (and then compete in swim meets
every single weekend, which explains the trunkful of T-shirts
in the attic emblazoned with slogans like WINNING IS CONTAGIOUS
and PAIN IS WEAKNESS LEAVING THE BODY). During vacation, they'd
have us do laps in the lake—to the float and back, ten times. Sufficiently tired out, we were less likely to cause mischief, bicker,
fight, especially at mealtimes, when we'd be too hungry to bother
with anything but eating.

The second chaos-suppressing tactic they employed was
the use of lists, more lists, and still more lists. Sometimes we'd
come downstairs in the morning and find a list with the heading
Boys' Jobs Today. Sometimes each of us had his *own* list. One at
a time we'd get through it, and one at a time the items would
be scratched off the list. My mother, too: She'd compose a list
for herself—near the bottom of that list there were always re-

minders about the things she had to get done for dinner. *Snap ends off beans. Boil eggs. Defrost steaks.* These too would slowly be eliminated, the tasks replaced by the subtle satisfaction of having everything in its proper place.

Here they come, Shalagh and the girls. The minivan rolls to a halt in the yard, and the girls burst forth. Their shirts are damp, and their mouths, interestingly, are stained crimson. The car's air-conditioning died in the hundred-degree weather, Shalagh explains, so they stopped about every twenty minutes to buy a fruit juice, a Gatorade—which meant they were soon stopping every ten minutes so the girls could use the restroom. Mother Nature, it would seem, is doing her best to make life difficult on everyone.

For lunch we're lakeside on the dock, and the necessary paraphernalia is laid out beside the smoking coals. Hands on hips, I consider the spread of utensils; it resembles the hardware a Viking surgeon would have carried into battle. Have I overdone it a bit? Though I'm equipped to skin and roast an ox, I'm merely preparing lunch for three adults and three children—Bermuda onions, cubes of cherry red pepper, chopped pork sausage with fennel seeds—and because I'm cooking for more than three, I'm focusing as intently as possible on not cutting myself; this may explain why, when lunch is just about ready, I reach, without the aid of a kitchen towel, for the iron frying pan that's crackling over the coals and seize the handle with my bare palm. There is a sound of bacon frying.

Consider the peripheral risks taken by the cook, especially one who routinely cooks for groups: cuts, burns, abrasions. Other injuries too, many having nothing to do with physical wounds—humiliation, stress. Isolation in a distant room. There were far fewer injuries in the days when I was single; it was no tragedy if dinner, poorly conceived, a vital preparatory step missed, took all night to prepare—which meant there was no hurry, no distraction, less built-in risk. Then again, those Saturday nights I passed drinking three martinis alone while watching samurai films didn't exactly qualify as happy times. Is it possible, I reason, that this isn't a binary dilemma? You could, after all, find a way to cook for a group *without* sending yourself to the emergency room.

If you'd prepared this lunch ahead of time, for example, right now you'd be sitting on the beach with your family, having a beer, enjoying the sun, and thinking about simply heating everything up. Instead, you're sitting lakeside with your badly burned palm dunked in the lake—and it's going to hurt tomorrow, and the next day. As with your discovery of the loneliness that can visit new parents, Keith, let's think of this discovery as *experience:* the thing you learned after it was too late. Maybe the better approach is to plan ahead and make one of those checklists your mom assembled every morning; tick things off one at a time, after they've fallen to the thock and thunk of chef's knife and cleaver. Or would you prefer to return to those days of cooking for one? I didn't think so. Cooking for your daughter, and for the people she brings into your home, isn't just teaching you to be a better parent. There are other gains to be had that have absolutely nothing to do with parenting, or even with what's on the table.

You want to be a happy man? Learn to cook family-style. And when you *do* drag the knife across your fingertip, don't lie to yourself and say that life used to be easier, saner, back in the days before you had Gracie and Jessica in your life, because it wasn't. (And you used to cut yourself *then*, too.) Alternatively, I'd recommend going with the logic printed on those T-shirts you used to wear at swim meets, while waiting your turn on the blocks:

NO PAIN, NO GAIN.

Family-Style Roasted Provençal Vegetables with Pernod-Tomato Compote

Serves 6 (as side dishes)

This one's fun. You make it way ahead of time, the action (both the roasted vegetables and the sauce) all happens in one pan, it's lovely to look at, and it's rustic as could be. Best of all, it uses Pernod—which gives me an excuse to keep a bottle around all the time. (Try adding 3 drops to a dry martini.) The parchment is necessary because it keeps the vegetables moist during roasting while allowing the liquid to slowly evaporate and concentrate.

If possible, buy squash, zucchini, tomatoes, and eggplant that all have roughly the same diameter—assembly is easier if the vegetables match up.

You can easily stretch this into a complete meal for a group by serving a store-bought rotisserie chicken alongside.

5 whole peeled canned tomatoes, drained and coarsely chopped

¼ cup diced red onion

¼ cup diced fennel (from about ½ small fennel bulb, cored, tough outer stalks peeled and discarded)

1 garlic clove, minced

1 sprig thyme

1 bay leaf

½ pound yellow squash, sliced into ¼-inch rounds

½ pound zucchini, sliced into ¼-inch rounds

½ pound fresh plum tomatoes, sliced into ¼-inch rounds

½ pound Italian eggplant, sliced into ¼-inch rounds

3 tablespoons Pernod or other anise-flavored liqueur

¼ cup chicken stock

¼ cup dry white wine

3 tablespoons extra virgin olive oil, plus more for drizzling

Salt and freshly ground black pepper

SPECIAL EQUIPMENT

High-sided, ovenproof 12-inch skillet, preferably iron

Parchment paper

Note: If making this recipe ahead, complete the recipe through step 3, allow to cool, cover the pan with foil, and refrigerate. To serve, lay the pan on the stovetop over medium heat, bring the sauce beneath the vegetables to a simmer, then continue with step 4.

1. Preheat the oven to 300° F.

2. Place a 12-inch skillet on the stovetop. Add the canned tomatoes, onion, fennel, garlic, thyme, and bay leaf. Stir them around so they're evenly distributed around the bottom of the pan. Beginning at the edge of the skillet, lay down a slice of yellow squash, then zucchini, then tomato, then eggplant, with the slices tightly overlapping. Repeat the series, moving around the perimeter of the skillet, then curling inside when you encounter the vegetables you started with, so that you get a coiled circle of overlapping vegetables that ends in the center of the skillet.

3. Drizzle the Pernod, stock, white wine, and oil over the tops of all the vegetables. Season the vegetables aggressively with salt and pepper. Cut out a parchment circle that covers the vegetables and lay it over the vegetables. Turn the heat under the skillet to high, and when the liquid in the bottom of the pan comes to a lively simmer, slide the pan into the oven. Roast for 90 minutes.

4. Remove the parchment paper and discard; place the skillet a few inches beneath the broiler and turn the broiler to high. Broil until the vegetables are nicely browned over all visible surfaces, even beginning to char at the tips; this can take 5 minutes or even longer, depending on the relative strength of the broiler. Serve directly from the pan while

still hot. Beneath each serving of vegetables you'll find a wonderfully sweet, concentrated, almost *jammy* tomato compote; spoon this over the vegetables (leaving the thyme sprig and bay leaf behind in the pan). Before serving, drizzle the vegetables with a little more olive oil.

Family-Style Roasted Cauliflower with Roasted Garlic Vinaigrette

Serves 6 (as side dishes)

Guests accustomed to eating cauliflower boiled until it falls apart will welcome this preparation. You can stretch this into a main course by tossing the finished cauliflower with cooked penne, chopped parsley, and a generous amount of extra virgin olive oil.

- ½ cup plus 2 tablespoons extra virgin olive oil
- 2 tablespoons chopped fresh thyme
- ¼ teaspoon pimentón (smoked paprika) or regular paprika
- 8 large unpeeled garlic cloves
- Salt and freshly ground pepper
- 3 large heads cauliflower, stalk sliced away and discarded, florets divided into large individual pieces and sliced in half
- 1 tablespoon white wine vinegar

Note: If making this recipe ahead, make the complete recipe, allow the cauliflower to cool, and place in a covered container in the refrigerator. To serve, either allow to come to room temperature, or warm for 5 minutes in a 350°F oven.

1. Preheat the oven to 425°F.
2. Pour 2 tablespoons of the oil onto a baking sheet and use your

hands to rub the oil over the entire surface of the sheet. Scatter 1 tablespoon of the thyme, 1/8 teaspoon of the pimentón, and 4 of the garlic cloves over the surface of the baking sheet, then season the entire sheet well with salt and pepper. Repeat with a second baking sheet. Place half the cauliflower on each baking sheet, placing the cut side of the floret down as you're able. Drizzle each sheet of cauliflower with 1 tablespoon of the oil.

3. Place the baking sheets in the oven and bake for 20 minutes. Take the sheets out of the oven and flip the florets so the cut side is facing up. Put the sheets back in the oven and bake for another 5 minutes. Turn the cauliflower once again, and bake a final 5 minutes.

4. Remove the cauliflower from the oven. Pick the garlic cloves out, separate the garlic from papery peels, and discard the peels. Combine the roasted garlic, the remaining ¼ cup olive oil and the white wine vinegar in a blender and puree. Place the cauliflower in a large serving dish (use 2 serving dishes, if necessary), pour the garlic vinaigrette over the cauliflower, and mix with your hands (or use a spoon, if the cauliflower is still too hot). Serve warm or at room temperature.

Family-Style Artichoke Frittata

Serves 6

Perfect for a brunch—you can have the frittata cooked and served, and the dishes you used to make it cleaned up, before your guests arrive. This frees you up to do more important things, like making mimosas.

> 8 large eggs
> 4 canned artichoke hearts, drained and thinly sliced
> 2 shallots, minced

2 teaspoons chopped fresh thyme, plus 4 to 5 sprigs, for garnish

1 tablespoon chopped fresh parsley

Salt and freshly ground black pepper

2 tablespoons unsalted butter

1 tablespoon olive oil

¼ cup freshly grated Parmesan cheese

Note: You can make this recipe an hour or more before serving—allow to rest at room temperature.

1. Place an oven rack 3 inches beneath the broiler and preheat the broiler.

2. In a large mixing bowl, briefly beat the eggs with a fork until just barely combined. Add the artichokes, shallots, chopped thyme, and parsley. Season well with salt and pepper, and stir.

3. Heat the butter and oil in a medium-sized nonstick skillet over medium-high heat. When the butter has melted and the foam just begins to subside, pour the egg mixture in the center of the pan and allow to cook undisturbed. In a few minutes the edges of the eggs will begin to set and puff up, while the center will still be raw. Allow to cook for another minute or two, until the center top is still very raw but beginning to set underneath.

4. Scatter the Parmesan evenly over the top of the eggs, then slide underneath the broiler. Broil the frittata until puffed up and cooked through, occasionally spinning or moving the pan so that the top browns evenly—continue broiling and moving the pan until the top is well browned all over and the frittata is cooked through, anywhere from 8 to 10 minutes total broiling. If the frittata looks like it's getting near to burning on top but is still uncooked in the middle (check by pressing gently in the center of the top—if it's not cooked through, you'll be able to feel soupy eggs hiding in the center), you can finish cooking it through on the stovetop over medium heat. You want that frittata to be very well browned, so don't shy away from pushing it under the broiler.

4. Remove from the oven and slide the frittata onto a cutting board. Garnish with fresh thyme sprigs, and serve—the frittata can rest for an hour or more at room temperature.

Roasted Chèvre Toasts

Serves 6 (as cocktail-party-size appetizers)

This recipe, more than any other I make, seems to be a favorite of groups. I serve these with wine before dinner, and more than a few people have felt compelled to ask if, with the next dinner, we might just have these and forget the rest of the meal.

> ½ pound goat cheese
> ¼ cup olive oil
> ½ teaspoon crushed red pepper flakes
> Salt and freshly ground black pepper
> Zest of ¼ lemon
> 1 tablespoon freshly squeezed lemon juice
> 4 large slices sourdough bread, about ¾ inch thick

Note: You can mix up the goat cheese mixture and even spread it on the bread ahead of time, but don't bake the toasts until you're ready to serve them—they're best eaten smoking hot.

1. In a small bowl, combine the cheese, oil, pepper flakes, salt and pepper, lemon zest, and lemon juice, and mash them together with a fork. You should have a thick goat cheese paste. Spread the mixture on each slice of bread, being careful to cover the entire top surface, especially the edges. (Exposed areas of bread will burn.) Spread it as thickly as you would peanut butter on a sandwich.

2. *To bake and serve:* Position one rack in the middle of the oven and one below it. Preheat the oven to 475°F. When ready to roast, lay the bread directly onto the top rack, tightly grouped, then slide the baking sheet onto the rack beneath to catch any cheese that drips down. Bake for 9 to 10 minutes—begin checking the toast at about 9 minutes, because some ovens burn hotter than others. You want the toasts to be a bit browned and bubbling on top and crispy throughout. Remove them from the oven, slice as you prefer, arrange on a platter, and serve immediately.

Sangre de Cocina

Serves 4 (as appetizers)

A perfect marriage of a traditional tomatillo salsa and guacamole. The tartness of the tomatillos gives the avocado a little extra punch. Wash your hands immediately after halving and scraping that jalapeño pepper or suffer the consequences.

> 1 tomatillo, husk peeled and discarded
>
> ½ medium onion
>
> 1 jalapeño pepper, halved, seeds and white ribs scraped away and discarded (or leave them in if you like a good amount of heat)
>
> 1 tablespoon peanut oil
>
> 2 avocados, peeled, pitted, and coarsely chopped
>
> ¼ cup fresh cilantro leaves
>
> Juice of 1 lime
>
> Salt

Note: You can make this ahead of time and refrigerate—to store, though, be sure to press plastic wrap directly down against the surface of the guacamole; this will prevent the surface from oxidizing and turning that unpleasant brown color.

1. Preheat the broiler to high. Place the tomatillo, onion, and the pepper halves on a baking sheet and rub with the oil (the onion and pepper halves should rest cut-side down). Broil until all are beginning to char a bit, about 5 minutes.

2. Place the tomatillo, onion, and pepper halves in a blender or food processor and add the avocados, cilantro, and lime juice. Season with salt. Pulse until coarsely pureed, scraping down the puree as necessary. Serve with tortilla chips.

the interesting case

July, and night is once again a bustling metropolis of wake-ups, with a rush hour that lasts from midnight to 6 a.m. I thought we had this *under control*—but no, every night Jessica and I are roused from sleep more times than we can count by a rattling, a raging, baby monitor. Days blend and blur together—Monday is Thursday is Sunday is Monday is Friday.

First it was reflux.

Now it's teeth—teeth have come into our lives, to murder sleep once again.

Gracie's upper and lower central incisors are coming in, arriving with all the implied threat of an advancing army, and they're not to be stopped, these little soldiers, so white and sharp in their enameled armature. The advance is a slow one too: This isn't some one- or two-night disruption, a lost weekend to recount at the water cooler on Monday. On the eleventh, or fifteenth, or nineteenth night in (I've lost count), I lift my head from the pillow and blink hard at the bookshelf. The baby monitor perched there is broadcasting a descending minor-key scale. I locate clothing and then teleport to Gracie's cribside to comfort her, to deliver the *necessary narcotic.** As I hoist her from her crib, I expect her to give me a look that says, *Oh, thank God it's you, Dad, here to comfort me.* But no, the look she gives me is *accusative,* a stinging paper cut to the heart. The look says, *Why can't you do something about this?* I respond with more Tylenol—a heavy-handed dose because, selfishly, I'm terrified that she'll begin to associate me with pain, and I remain with her in the dark as I wait for the Tylenol to take effect.

Gracie pushes back from my chest with both palms and studies my face.

I open my mouth and show her my teeth.

She hesitates, then reaches out and touches them—incisor, canine, molar.

"Teeth," I say. "You have them."

Then she opens her mouth and shows me *her* teeth.

I lean close and study the little horizontal slices, the enamel a lunar blue in the darkness. (What dreams dentists must have, to look at teeth all day this way.) The teeth are telling me that biology has an agenda of its own and that it will pitilessly advance its own aims. This needn't be a bad thing, biology's interest in my daughter's future. I only wish the process didn't involve so much pain.

When life becomes challenging, we reach for a resolution; if a resolution isn't available, a coping tool will do. Jessica and I adopt the same strategy we seized when she decided she wanted to go for a drug-free birth. "It's temporary," she says, "just a stage," and I nod and say, "Yes, it's temporary. Just a stage." Pretty soon we're nodding at each other like a couple of bobblehead dolls, agreeing that it's *just temporary,* even though it already seems to

---

* No, really, I seem to have gained the ability to teleport from place to place. I wake in bed to the redlining baby monitor and then, with the decisive dislocation of a cinematic *cut,* find that I'm cribside, with no recollection at all of the walk to Gracie's room.

have gone on for quite a long time. We talk to friends by phone. We email and text, and play ping-pong with this convenient logic. "It's temporary, just a stage," we say, over cell and land-line, and we text, *Tmprry, jst a stg*, and e-mail *Temporary, just a stage.* But the mazy nighttime roundabouts continue, the teeth in their implacable advance, accompanied by the accusative look. I'm teleporting from place to place; I'm dosing out Tylenol like a schoolyard pusher. Are we really going to try this again, this *tem-porary* thing, when it didn't work the first time? But this is what parents must do to cope: You rely on the tropes at hand, and somehow they get you through. The lesson this time round is the same it was the first time: *Temporary* is a relative term, and it's maddeningly open-ended. You don't know if it will last a day or a week or a month or even longer. At least this stage is dependable: If reflux was a whodunit, teeth prove to be more of a whenwillit. You don't go to bed wondering if you're going to awaken to the sound of the baby crying. You go to bed wondering when and how many times and for how long.

There *is* an upside to all this dreary news about sleep and pain—Gracie has become preternaturally excited about eating solid foods, not the usual purees but the authentic, unmashed ar-ticle. It's as if she's realized that she's leaped about seven rungs on the food chain. Suddenly I'm able to cook, really *cook* for her, challenge myself rather than restrain myself—I fry things up and sling them in front of her still warm and entirely unmodi-fied, the sole Milanese proving to be a mere test run for some flash plates of fish and chips, grilled cheese, veal schnitzel. Jes-sica and I have beer-battered fish tacos for dinner; the next day I present a piece of the leftovers to Gracie for lunch and watch with more than a little awestruck amusement as she seizes the crispy fish and bites down. I'm underslept and despairing for my nights, but during the day, during meals, I experience a certain lightening of spirits. My daughter is eating exactly what we ate the night before, with no modifications. I'm no longer planning meals that can be transformed into a child's meal, because no transformation is necessary.

What we have here is a baby who has weaponized herself, apparently preparing for a long and healthy life. A once four-pound baby now fiercely growing and even wrenching fish from my hand. I find comfort in fresh evidence of the resilience of biology, in the idea that you *can* turn things around—and we have teeth, at least in part, to thank for the change. We're moving from strength to strength at last, and because of that I'm able to forgive her teeth for what they've done to her, and to our sleep.

A looping video of the NICU plays in my mind's eye, like some dreadful art exhibit on the nature of fear. For the better part of a year, I've done my best to avert my eyes from it, to avoid thinking about what it all meant.

Now, ten months in, with teeth literalizing my daughter's move from weakening newborn to thriving baby, I finally have the courage to revisit the memory reel, to face up to exactly what I was thinking as those events were unfolding.

The character who plays me in this reel, the spirit haunting the waiting room, is always preparing himself for the worst possible outcome. He's doing this because the previous seven months *taught* him to prepare for the worst, to see things in the unkindest light.

It wasn't just the early delivery that was the problem, you see. During our pregnancy there was bad news, and then more bad news, and then more bad news. It all worked out in the end—I'm here, Jessica is here, and Gracie is here. Cooking for Gracie has become my way of asserting, daily, that these frightening experiences are behind us, that my daughter, who was born so very, very light, is eating and growing and will continue to eat and grow. This story is a success story, in which all the principals lived. But for a time there it didn't much look like things were going to work out that way.

Three months into the pregnancy, a genetic counselor called to tell us that a test we'd taken showed an anomaly; it was likely that our baby had a bad genetic malformation. So we had *more* tests. A few weeks later, at work, my phone rang—it was Jessica, with the results of the second round of tests, and she was practically mute with confusion and fear. Our baby didn't have the genetic malformation they'd first suspected—the test had revealed something much, much worse. Chorionic villus sampling had given a positive marker for the real whammy, a head clutcher called full trisomy 16.

A question naturally followed: What is full trisomy 16? I typed out a few keys on the keyboard. The first page that came up told me that trisomy 16 is a genetic disorder. And then I read: *Full trisomy 16 is not compatible with life.* As if on cue, sweat burst from my every pore.

From there, the conversation, tinged with unreality, went something like:

Keith: What did she tell you?
Jessica: She said it was all decided.

Keith: Decided how?
Jessica: She said, you've already passed the baby by now. Of course.

I tried to parse just what Jessica was trying to tell me, and it didn't take me long to get it: I was being told that the experts involved believed my baby should already be gone.

But you have to hold it together at work. I set down my pencil. I rotated my chair away from a colleague sitting at the desk to my right. I put my face in my right hand.

Keith: And you said—
Jessica: And I said, No, we haven't.

Keith: And then—
Jessica: And then the counselor said, You haven't?

Keith: And you said—
Jessica: And I said, No, we haven't. Is that odd? And she said—

Keith: And she said—
Jessica: And she said, Well, yes, it is, because as far as we know, it's one hundred percent fatal by the twelfth week of the pregnancy.

We were at the fifteenth week.

My father, now a retired oncologist, had a physician friend who once said, "You never want to be the interesting case"—the point being that you want to be the thing the doctor has seen a thousand times, because that means everything's going to work out, and work out according to an established plan. But no, we were now a case no one had ever heard of—including another friend of my father's who is the director of genetic medicine at a major university. Suddenly we were the *interesting case* and remained the interesting case for a very long time, because it turned out (after a battery of further tests in which Jessica was again poked and prodded like a pincushion, and I learned, too late, that what you do during these tests is look away from the sonogram monitor, because *you don't want to get attached to that baby*)—it turned out that what made us the *interesting case* was that the baby's placenta had this malformation, but our baby did not. Somehow, the embryo had got this malformation, and Gracie, when she became a fetus, had thrown it off into the thing that would cloak and feed and protect her for the remainder of the pregnancy.

Here things appeared to be resolved. And they most certainly were not. That experience really was just the opening of an epic composed of many chapters, complete with moments of suspense, fear, surprise, and betrayal, in which we learned all sorts of things about bone length, fetal weight in utero, the ability of the placenta to deliver blood and nutrients, et cetera. My cumulative memory of the pregnancy, a composite of the many crushing moments of dashed hope, is of sitting in a plush office while a trusted doctor shakes his head and says, "Things don't look good."

Oh man, what a secret *crybaby* I turned into during these weeks and months. *Things don't look good*, the composite memory said, and I responded in kind. Each night I'd put Jessica to bed, snap off the light, pull the covers up to her chin, and then go back out to the living room to watch some television—and then an ad would appear onscreen showing a chuckling baby pat-pat-patting a table with fat little hands, and suddenly oh boohoohoo, and I would look at my reflection in the dark window glass and see that my face was wet with tears. Is it possible to mourn someone you've never met, someone you've never spoken to, someone you've never touched? I'd try to tell myself, Everything's going to work out, but when I'd open my mouth to reassure myself, my nerves would strain into the silence like violin strings, and all that would come out was more oh boohoohoo.

We're trying to *get it all in* here—the whole truth—so now, on the page, I must revisit that moment when we were sent home from the hospital after that early morning false start on the day Gracie was born, the contractions having been stopped by an IV. In that moment, what I was thinking was: I have only five more weeks of allowing myself to believe that my baby will live. And then the truth will come tumbling down from its terrible height. *The placenta won't hold up through the birth. There will be a hemorrhage. And then we'll lose the kid.* We arrived at our apartment, I put Jessica to bed, and, because she was hungry, I made her a grilled cheese. As I handed the plate to her, I felt as if I were giving her a gift—a gift that was a way of saying, *Thanks, thanks for keeping my baby alive for another day. Thanks for being the only safe place she has had all this time. You are the only safe place anymore.*

The truth is that I didn't ever allow myself to believe that my baby would live, and when Jessica ran hollering into the bathroom and leaped, fully dressed, into the shower with me—the image that will burn in my mind's eye in the moment before my own death—a significant part of me accepted that it was possible we were headed not to the birth of our first child but rather toward that terrible thing that is the opposite of birth.

It all worked out. She's here, and now her teeth are in.

July is behind us. In just a few days, Gracie will be eleven months old. Four weeks later, I'll be the father of a one-year-old girl—one who's certainly not a newborn, and not a baby anymore either, not really. And on that day I'll remind myself to cherish the milestone, because there were a few moments back there when it didn't look like we'd make it.

Simple dinner tonight for Gracie—appropriate to the season. Once again, repurposed from what Jessica and I had last night. Cherry tomatoes peeled but left whole, and tossed with a little salt to marinate. Sautéed half coins of yellow squash, Spanish onion, loads of good olive oil—all of it twirled together with cappellini and a handful of chopped just-off-the-stalk mint, with a good dusting of quality pecorino to finish up.

I consider the tangle of pasta on my cutting board; I *could* chop it all up into paste, but why bother? She's got the teeth she needs to do the job herself.

I hand the plate over and sit next to her as I watch her dig in.

She picks up a tomato and looks to me, unsure of how to proceed.

"Go ahead," I say, showing her. "Use your teeth. You don't need my help."

And as she takes a bite I feel as if we're somehow pushing back against all those forces that were fighting us. Perspective has arrived. I used to think I was alone in confronting those forces, but the teeth make me feel as if my daughter is somehow conspiring with me.

So I will take the lack of sleep, the labyrinth of wake-ups we walk every night, the teleporting from place to place. I will happily greet the ghost in the mirror at daylight—after all, *it's temporary, just a stage*—if becoming well acquainted with him is the price to be paid for this reversal of fortune, and its attendant regeneration of faith.

Spaghetti with Yellow Squash, Cherry Tomatoes, Mint, and Pecorino

Serves 2 adults and 1 child

If you feel like putting on a show, buy cherry tomatoes on the vine and clip the tomatoes off with scissors, leaving a half-inch of vine attached throughout. Looks great on the plate.

15 or so cherry tomatoes

½ teaspoon salt, plus more for seasoning

½ pound dried spaghetti or other dried pasta

4 tablespoons extra virgin olive oil

½ medium onion, chopped

1 large yellow squash, halved and sliced into thin half-moons

Freshly ground black pepper

½ cup dry white wine

3 tablespoons (packed) chopped fresh mint

½ cup freshly grated pecorino cheese

Note: Before serving this to your child, make sure she's already tried all the primary ingredients and has shown no allergic reaction.

1. Bring a large pot of salted water to a boil over high heat. Score a tiny *X* in the flower end of the tomatoes. Drop the tomatoes in the boiling water and cook for about 15 seconds, until the skins begin to loosen. Remove from the water with a slotted spoon and immediately place under cold running water. Strip the skins off and discard, then place the tomatoes in a bowl and toss with the salt. Allow the tomatoes to marinate for 15 minutes, then go ahead with the rest of the recipe.

2. Add the spaghetti to the boiling water and cook according to the directions on the package.

3. While the spaghetti is cooking, heat the oil in a large skillet over medium-high heat. Add the onion and sauté until soft, about 4 minutes. Add the squash and sauté until the squash too is softened, about 3 minutes. Season with salt and pepper. Add the wine and simmer gently until the pasta is ready.

4. When the spaghetti has finished cooking, drain it, and then add it to the pasta sauce. Pour the tomatoes, and any juice that has accumulated under them, into the spaghetti. Simmer the spaghetti an additional minute in the skillet, turning it in the sauce, then remove the skillet from the heat. Add the mint, ¼ cup of the cheese, combine well, then divide onto plates, setting some aside for a child's meal. Serve immediately, passing the remaining cheese at the table.

Fish Tacos

Serves 4 adults and 1 child

Surfer-dude food that's good for the soul in the same way that, well, surfing is. With this recipe, you harness the simple beauty of one of nature's great inventions—the fish—and pair it with the simple beauty of one of mankind's great inventions—the tortilla. I recommend corn tortillas, if you can get your hands on them, over flour tortillas.

> 1 cup flour
>
> 1 cup beer
>
> Peanut or vegetable oil, for frying
>
> 1 egg white
>
> Pinch of salt
>
> 1 pound skinless Pacific Cod fillet, rinsed, dried, and sliced into 3 × 1-inch strips
>
> 8 corn or flour tortillas
>
> 6 shredded radishes
>
> 2 cups shredded red cabbage
>
> ½ cup sour cream
>
> ¼ cup coarsely chopped fresh cilantro
>
> 4 lime wedges, for serving

Note: Before serving this to your child, make sure she's already tried white flaky fish with no allergic reaction. Make sure the peanut oil isn't a problem, either, before serving.

1. Preheat the oven to 350°F. Whisk the flour and beer together and allow to sit, covered, at room temperature for 1 hour. (Allow the egg white to rest at room temperature for an hour beside the flour-beer mixture—if the egg isn't at room temperature, you're going to have a devil of a time getting it to whip into soft peaks.)

2. Heat 2 inches of oil in a large dutch oven to 350°F. Place the egg white in a large mixing bowl, add the salt, and whisk vigorously until soft peaks form. Gently fold the egg whites into the beer batter with a spatula. Drop the fish pieces in the batter.

3. Wrap the stack of tortillas tightly in foil and place them in the

oven while you're preparing the fish—they should bake for about 10 minutes total.

4. Increase the heat to high under the oil—when it reaches 375°F, lay 4 or 5 battered fish pieces gently in the oil (don't overcrowd the pan—a standard dutch oven should hold about 4 pieces at a time). Fry until golden brown all over, turning pieces occasionally in the oil, about 4 minutes, depending on how well the oil retains its heat. Set cooked fish pieces on a roasting rack to drain while you fry the next batch.

5. The tortillas should finish warming while you're cooking the fish. If you aren't finished with the fish when the tortillas are done with their 10-minute bake, just take them out of the oven and let rest still wrapped in the foil.

6. If desired, quickly rewarm the first batch of fish pieces in the hot oil before serving. To serve, place a warm tortilla on a plate—top with a small handful of radish and cabbage. Lay a few pieces of fried fish on top and dot with a good dollop or two of sour cream and a pinch of cilantro. Serve immediately with a wedge of lime on each plate to squeeze over the fish. (Turn leftovers into a meal for your baby by allowing her to dip crispy fish pieces into sour cream.)

arrivals

I'm crisscrossing the sidewalk outside a Spanish wine and tapas bar just off Union Square, hiking the baking sidewalk beneath the steady gaze of the sun. You know me and have seen me before: I'm the grinning guy hunched forward over his toddling half-pint. Beads of sweat run down my jaw and gather trembling at my chin, soon to fall to the sidewalk, where they evaporate almost instantly. The wine bar to my right is one of my favorite restaurants on the planet, and my jaw tightens as I think of the *pan con tomate* I *could* be eating right now at one of its dark-wood communal tables were I inside—I'd chase it with a *copita* of sherry, maybe an espresso to close. Get the bill and head out into the afternoon skating on a light midday buzz of sherry fumes and caffeine, just the sort to propel you through a day where above all you know that you are *just not going to get a nap.*

It's not in the cards, that *pan con tomate.*

Nor is the nap. Not anytime soon, at least.

I lift my gaze and peer through the glass shop front into the cool, dark interior of the bar. Jessica is there on the far side of the glass. She is equally amused and nonplussed, sipping a Navarran rosé as she waits for her beet salad to arrive.

She waves to me, then lifts her eyebrows and shrugs, as if to say, *What can we do?*

I telegraph the question back in the declarative. It's all I can do—I can't wave back because Gracie is gripping my index fingers tightly with her fists, and if I take one away to wave she's going to topple to the ground. She's using my hands as stabilizer bars while she strides up and down, up and down, up and down the sidewalk. Gracie is largely innocent of all this parental telegraphy, obsessed, as she is, by this new talent of hers. The talent seems to have shorted out the geopositioning tool in her brain, causing it to send messages that tell her *Go, and it doesn't matter where.* Walk east? OK, let's walk east. Now west? West it is. Have we been here before? *It doesn't matter. Walking is fun.* Walking is fun for me, too, though after the fourth or fifth pass over the same stretch of sidewalk I begin to think longingly of that *pan con tomate* again. It's going to be a while before I get any.

A friend once told me, "She's really starting to give back" when I asked how things were going with his own daughter, then three. All his hard work, he said, was beginning to pay off in signs of affection and love from his child. Jessica and I aren't there yet. The excitement of this stage of Gracie's life is found in the new developments, in the surprise we get in watching our infant daughter evolve slowly into a young girl. There's plenty of this excitement—but I have to confess that there is very little *giving back* right now. The rewards have become fewer and sparser, in fact, now that Gracie has realized there is an exciting world out there, one that she can traverse and explore and discover. Her attentions, once directed so fiercely toward me and her mother, are now directed outward, and we can only travel with her and hope to be a part of the experience.

Five, six more laps, and I've had enough. My damp shirt sticks to my back as I steer Gracie toward the wine bar and hip-check open the door. A blast of superchilled air washes over me like a benediction. Jessica is already sliding off her stool to take a shift.

Her beet salad's just arrived, but there's no time, so she forks down one quick mouthful, then takes over.

And then I find that I'm nearly alone, in a nearly silent room. This doesn't happen often. I hold Jessica's cold glass briefly to the back of my neck, enjoy the peaceful quiet. My only company is the pair of staff behind the wood bar. They chat quietly in Spanish as they polish glasses with white towels. One of them looks up and asks if I'll be having something to drink.

I will. I would very much enjoy a *copita* of the Alvaer.

And will I have something to eat?

I will. The *pan con tomate* would be wonderful.

The waiter approaches, slides the *copita* of sherry to my elbow. Linen napkins, silverware against dark wood. Handsome place, the menu hand-lettered on the giant mirror behind the wide bar. I want to eat my last meal here, and every meal until then. I don't ever want to leave. I lift the pale straw-colored sherry and have a sip, and in a single instant I'm fired more than twenty years back in time, to the first evening of a hot summer I spent in northern Spain with my older brother, Geoff. That first night, the eldest sister of the host family I was staying with brought me to a restaurant for a very late *merienda*, and as I was still deciding if I was up to the challenge of living in this unfamiliar setting, she and her friend ordered me a simple *fino*, along with a plate of fried seafood. I took my first sip of the *fino*—already marveling that I, a sixteen-year-old, could drink alcohol at a restaurant—and was silenced by the pleasantly unfamiliar taste. Then I tried a bite of the fried seafood—it was much too hot from the fryer, but I was so hungry I couldn't wait. It was so good, so good. I asked her in Spanish what I was eating. "*Calamares*," she said. I told her I didn't know that word. She grinned and raised her hands, wrists together, and waved all ten of her fingers at once, and I tried not to panic. This is why you travel, after all: to do things you've never done before.

The trip was a freak piece of luck that came our way, an opportunity to join an American swim team in Santander. The workouts were deadly, four hours a day in the pool, and sometimes dinner, the traditionally lighter *cena*, was nothing more than slices of salami and Catalán cheese with bread, and a few apricots to share after the meal. I was swimming as many as ten thousand meters a day during those four hours of practice, burning calories the way a furnace eats fuel, and my body had slowly begun to devour itself. I had always been a thinnish kid, but not this way, to a degree that I could count my ribs. I woke with the hunger every morning and carried it with me all through the day and into the night again, a hunger so strong that it seemed you could eat and eat and never be sated again; and of course the good quality of the food only left me wishing there were more of it. I soon began to understand the usefulness of bread, the way it pushed the hunger back just a fraction more than other foods. On good days, my host family mother made Spanish tortilla, which had no relation to the Mexican tortillas I knew from home—it was more like a quiche of onions and potatoes that had been fried in oil. I ate every speck she gave me, wiping the plate with a piece of bread—the bread helped it almost meet the collective need—and then lay in bed afterward ignoring my rumbling stomach and wondering how long one can live on too few calories.

Near the end of the stay my host family and I traveled to the rural outskirts of Torrelavega to visit the host father's favorite uncle. Tío, I was told, had lived in New York City for ten years following the Great Depression, and wished to speak English with me. I was nervous to meet him. Like all Castillians whose English wasn't that good, he would mix his poor English with a great deal of rapid Castillian Spanish, with a *th* sound in place of every *c*, and I would spend most of the night three or four sentences behind. After five solid years of study, and an entire summer of speaking Spanish every day, my grasp of the language was excellent, but of course it was classroom Spanish, a million miles removed from the real conversational thing. Tío wore a tweed cap and suit and looked very young for his age, though the hand-rolled cigarettes

he smoked nonstop had yellowed his fingers and had given him a
cough that sounded like someone shaking a sheet of aluminum. I
was astonished to see that he could roll a cigarette without looking at his hands. The father insisted that I sit with Tío and talk
with him, in English, about the United States. Tío seemed only
too happy to tell me about his experience there, though his English was extremely weak and he soon segued back into Spanish.
When I shifted into Spanish, to match him, the father called from
the next room, saying, "English, speak English with him." So we
resumed our conversation in two languages.

After our formal conversation was finished, Tío rolled another
cigarette and told me, in Spanish, a truly sad story about a friend
in New York City who'd been knifed to death for refusing to pay
protection to the Mafia; soon after his friend was killed, Tío received
news that his father was gravely ill, and he returned home to care
for him. When his father died, Tío, as the eldest son, assumed the
responsibility of supporting the family, and his chance to return to
America was lost. He regretted leaving for the rest of his life, he
said, and had never got past the sense of having lived an incom-
plete life. It was very hard following along once the story was in full
swing, though his eyes helped. I've tried to write the story many different times since, but it always comes out like a talentless retelling
of Hemingway's "The Killers" and is never as sad in the retelling as
it was the day Tío told it to me. I know regret, but I don't think I
know regret that way, and I sometimes think that telling stories like
that one requires a hunger beyond that which I understand.*

Of all the things I experienced that summer, though, it's not
the memory of Tío's story that gnaws at me the most. While

* On my way out the door, he stopped me and said a line that I still can't believe I
was allowed to hear: "Give my regards," he said, "to the Statue of Liberty." He *actually said it,* this line that would cause even the most mawkish Hollywood writer to
groan aloud and reach for the delete button. The thing about a cliché is that it's
an expression with no feeling behind it, borrowed from elsewhere—a cliché is a
secondhand emotion. And that just wasn't what was happening here. The words,
in his mouth, were the *opposite* of a cliché.

walking up the jetway at Logan at the end of the trip, I looked up and saw a person jumping up and down with excitement on the far side of a window marked ARRIVALS. I thought, That person is very, very excited to see someone. And then I realized that this person was my mother, who was unable to control her excitement at having us back. It was like being shaken by the collar, this sudden splashdown in my familiar environment: I had, I realized, been gone all winter and spring at boarding school, then had vanished for most of the summer in Spain. The number of days I'd spent home in the previous year could be counted on my fingertips. My parents, put simply, had given up time with their children so that we could have the experience of a lifetime. My memories of Spain have vividly endured. But then so has that image of my mother jumping up and down on the far side of the glass. It's an image I often revisit when I'm finding the pressures of parenting draining, those days when you think: I cannot take another moment of this sacrifice. I just want to walk away, alone.

The Spanish have a saying, "You can do anything you want in life, but you have to pay the bill before you're through." The logic being, You want to go on an all-night bender? Go ahead. Just be ready for the terrible moment of waking at first light. You want to cheat on your taxes, steal from the neighbor? Do it. But don't weep and moan when the law knocks on your door. You want to run out on your wife and kids? Go right ahead. And when, years later, they turn down that opportunity to reconnect with you, don't bother pointing fingers anywhere but at the person in the mirror. You knew what you were getting into.

With parenting, I think what happens is that you pay the bill *first*—and that's why the price cuts so deeply. You give, but everything you give is just an investment in a future, and you never know how it's going to pay out—your only choice is to fork it over and hope for the best. *She's really starting to give back,* that friend told me, and I'm beginning to understand. You give by giving up yourself and hope that it comes back to you.

The sherry is already half gone when, a few minutes later, the *pan con tomate* arrives, bread perfectly charred, rubbed with fresh garlic and a tomato half, the surface given a quick dusting of salt and a whiplash of quality olive oil just before being served. I pick up one of the thick slices of bread, still hot to the touch.

And the front door opens. Jessica walks in, awkwardly hip-checking the door open as best she can, unable to use her hands because Gracie is gripping her index fingers, using them as stabilizers. She's bent over almost double, her neck is glossy with sweat, and she looks as if she could use a break.

"Take a turn?" she asks.

But I'm already rising from my stool and reflecting on another Spanish saying appropriate to the reflective mood: *Dime con quién andas y te diré quién eres.* Tell me with whom you walk, and I'll tell you who you are.

Is it really so big a sacrifice, to have to wait? There is hunger, after all, and then there is hunger; and if the sort you have can be pushed back with bread, count yourself lucky.

Pan con Tomate Sandwiches with Serrano Ham

Serves 2 to 3

This, incidentally, is my favorite recipe in the entire book. There is nothing better than a slice of *pan con tomate*—except, maybe, 2 slices of *pan con tomate,* with some serrano ham (it's what prosciutto wishes it could be) sandwiched between. Make sure your bread slices are thick; if sliced too thin, the toasted bread will turn brittle, when what you're after is toast that's crisp on the outside, but still yielding and soft inside.

> 6 thick slices crusty country or sourdough bread
>
> 6 tablespoons extra virgin olive oil
>
> 2 large garlic cloves
>
> Salt and freshly ground black pepper
>
> 3 tomatoes, halved horizontally
>
> 9 thin slices serrano ham or prosciutto

1. Place an oven rack a few inches beneath the broiler and preheat the broiler. Brush both sides of the bread slices with 2 tablespoons of the oil, then place the bread beneath the broiler. Broil until very well browned, then flip the bread and broil the second side well, too, until little bits of char begin to show.

2. Lay the bread slices on a serving platter, and immediately, while the bread is still very hot, rub the surface of each slice well with a garlic clove. Drizzle the remaining 4 tablespoons of oil over the bread slices, then season each slice with salt and pepper. Rub the tops of each bread slice with a tomato half, gently squeezing the tomato to release the tomato juice and seeds onto the surface of the bread. Discard tomato half, or save for another use.

3. Lay 3 slices of serrano ham on one slice of bread, then top with another slice of bread, tomato side facing the serrano ham. Repeat to make 3 sandwiches total. Serve while still very hot to the touch.

doing time

Here in the midst of vacation, I'm just waiting to return to work so I can get some rest, because it turns out that time off as the parents of a child who can crawl and stand is an awful lot more work than vacationing as the parents of a child who cannot. Time off as the parents of a child who can crawl and stand, in fact, feels an awful lot like time on the clock.

This truism never occurred to me in all those weeks and months I had to prepare for crawling. This is how reliable my radar is. In early June, during our first summer trip to New Hampshire, we'd walk down to the lake late in the morning, plunk Gracie down on a blanket in the shade, swipe her face with sunblock, cover her head with a sun hat, surround her with fourteen books, two stuffed animals, a plastic pot and shovel, and a handful of dry-docked floaty toys, and then Jessica and I would sit in the sun and read. An hour later, Gracie's blanket would subside to a creeping band of sunlight; we'd move her, and everything would start all over again. This is pretty much what we did all day, every day, for a week. But on the first morning of our second trip to New Hampshire, I discover that things are going to be different this time around.

I plunk Gracie down on a blanket in the shade, swipe her face with sunblock, cover her head with a sun hat, surround her with fourteen books, two stuffed animals, a plastic pot and shovel, and a handful of dry-docked floaty toys, and then sit in the sun, planning to read for an hour. The moment I sit down, Gracie gets to her hands and knees and begins to crawl toward the edge of the dock at top speed. I leap up from my chair and snatch her away from the edge just as she's about to tumble headlong into the lake. I try the same setup again, this time with one cunning defensive tactic—I sit between Gracie and the edge of the dock. My plan falls into disarray, however, when she crawls toward the *other* side of the dock. My kid is a genius. So I leap up, et cetera, et cetera. We have a problem here. We're on vacation, but suddenly vacation is looking like it's going to be anything but restful. Suddenly vacation is looking like it's going to be a lot like work.

Forever the optimist, I try another tactic. I flip four benches on their sides and assemble them in an enclosed ring around Gracie's blanket, constructing a sort of infant minimum-security prison. And when I see the vexed look on my daughter's face, I feel that warm rush you get in knowing you've outsmarted your eleven-month-old. Then Gracie pulls herself up to standing (at this early stage she wobbles like a drunk), hooks her leg over the edge of the bench, and flips herself bodily onto the dock. Tears, blood, et cetera, et cetera. I am a bad dad, a bad dad.

Gracie, by the way, is bald—and not just *sort of bald*, or *kind of bald*, or any of those other generous euphemisms people use. Our Gracie, never content to do anything halfway, is anarchically, enthusiastically bald, and it's looking as if she's going to stay that way for quite a while. At this point, defying all odds and genetic signposts, I have managed to hold on to my hair, which means that baldness, and its uneasy relationship with the blazing summer sun overhead, is a subject this family knows little about. Jessica has remembered to bring along something like seventeen hats—pink ones and white ones and blue ones, some with duckies and some with froggies and some with paisley designs, and even one made of fabric that resembles a pair of shorts I had during the preppie heydays of the eighties. Unfortunately, although we've remembered to arm ourselves and our bald baby with sun-thwarting hats, we've discovered that it's damn near impossible to convince Gracie to leave them on her head for more than five seconds. During the previous visit she was in the shade all day, so the hat-removal thing wasn't really a problem. Now, when we put the hat on her head, she not only immediately removes it, but also crawls out of the shade and into the sunlight, where the September sun begins doing its sun thing. I put the hat back on. She takes it off. I put it on. She takes it off. Insanity is sometimes defined as doing the same thing over and over expecting a different result. If that is a true definition, you could accurately state that during the first days of vacation I was clinically insane. Finally we realize that one of the hats has a strong Velcro strap beneath the chin that secures the hat to her head in a way that takes her at least a minute or two to undo.

There's also the matter of sand, which, true to sand's accepted nature, finds its way into *everything*—the novels I page through on the dock always retain a tablespoon or two in their spines, even months later, and my Chekhov paperback will pour its grainy treasure in my lap as I revisit it for a light midwinter read. The trunk of our car is about halfway toward being a sandbox of its own. Poor Gracie is sleeping on a dune in her Pack 'n Play. The only time of day she gets cranky is in the afternoon, after lunch, when we give up on our minimum-security prison on the dock and move to water's edge, where she waves to ducks, pats the lake water, and somehow shovels about two handfuls of sand directly into her diaper. We herd her into the shower, and, holding her up into the stream, try to get the sand out of the little baby-fat folds, but we soon learn that sand, when set in place by sunblock, is notoriously good at sticking in place.

Seeking a midweek change of scenery, we travel for a day to the Maine coast—to the end of America, or the beginning, depend-

ing on how you see things. There Mother Nature reveals that she
has a sense of humor, dials the temperature down to the low six-
ties, and mushes whipping winds down on us—apparently from
somewhere in northern Canada. When churned up by the whipping wind, the sand *here* makes for a wincing experience, but the
hot eye of the sun sparkles off the infinity of ocean and invests
what might otherwise be an oppressive morning with a festive,
can-do overtone (plus I find that a visit to the ocean hits some
sort of internal reset button in my consciousness, refreshing me
as a night of deep-dreaming does).

So it is a cold morning we pass at the coast. Gracie, at first
decked out in a fetching two-piece bikini, is soon mummified in a
onesie, long-sleeve shirt, hat, and a pair of fuzzy socks that reach
halfway up her thighs. Mom opts for similar dress and Jackie O.
sunglasses, while Dad butches it out in board shorts and sweatshirt.
Both parents, anesthetized by heavenly bites of lobster and crab roll
(and two illegally smuggled Heinekens), chase Gracie around as
best they can but are mostly preoccupied with keeping the whipping sand out of their french fries. By the end of it, Gracie resembles a mad aerobics instructor rolled in sugar, which makes for an
interesting cleanup in the parking lot, the fix based largely around
a handful of wipes, a liter of bottled water, a naked, kicking child
held aloft, and two soaked but well-fed parents, who return home
windburned but strangely reenergized for a final day of vacation.

Wildlife and spiders are the true year-round residents of the cabin;
we're merely interlopers. (A favorite late-night pursuit is to flip on
the spotlight just outside the screened-in porch and watch the rows
of hummingbird-sized spiders scramble to haul in their gyrating
catch of dinner—with any luck, the mosquitoes who plan to dine
on you *tomorrow* night). I grill dinner almost every night we're up
in New Hampshire—a rosemary-smoked steak, beer-can chicken,

garlic shrimp *a la plancha*—because I love the grill and don't have access to one in New York. As I stand amid a cloud of mosquitoes, cooking and swatting and turning and slapping and wincing over my dinner, the mosquitoes making dinner out of *me*, I sometimes begin to identify with the spiders (hence the habit of flipping on the spotlight and watching the spiders get to work—we do this because we're rooting for them). This matter of identifying with the spiders takes some time, though, considering the persistence and omnipresence of those eight-legged beauties—it can be quite a shock, that first morning of vacation, to awake, roll over, and find an *Araneus cavaticus* clinging with eight legs to your bedside water glass. On that first morning, my response to this discovery is uniformly violent, swift, and lethal. But by the third or fourth morning my response is more along the lines of, Hey, spider, how did you sleep, man? And did you eat well last night? And then I roll over and go back to bed. After all, it's more *his* place than mine. I come to fit my environment very nicely in a matter of days.

Still, there remains, on the last morning, the unresolved environmental matter of the infant minimum-security prison, which is now loaded with books, toys, plastic pots, and about a bushel of sand. Gracie continues to resist accepting that *these are her boundaries*. Here's what she does: She waits until I sit down at a distance of a few feet and then she pulls herself standing, hooks a leg over the edge of the benches, and attempts an escape. I get up, rescue her with about half a second to spare (I'm getting good at this), get her situated again with a book or plastic pot, wait until she appears to be fully absorbed, then go sit down. At this point she pulls herself standing, hooks a leg, et cetera. If this sounds repetitive, rest assured that this is a five-minute period of a seven-day vacation.

Gracie, I ask, are you ever going to stay put?

She hooks her leg over the bench and glares at me.

Are you?

Dee, dee, dee, dee, dee, she says, wobbling like a drunk trying to scale a fence.

As I consider the four or five hours remaining today, I'm reminded of something someone told me the night Gracie was born—the same hour she was born, in fact. Two nurses had been assigned to care for Jessica after the birth, but it soon became apparent that the two nurses were dear friends and were really just excited to have some time to talk with each other and interview the new parents. The interview stalled soon after they arrived, when one of the nurses announced that her leg had gone numb (pinched nerve, long story), so I volunteered my seat. She took it, I leaned against the windowsill, and there we were, four people all sort of caring for each other, a little human interaction going on, a little warm glow developing in the room after all the drama of the evening. The nurse without the numb leg asked how big our daughter was. Four pounds, we told her, and she shook her head and said, "Woo, watch out for those little ones," implying that nature hardwires the little ones to find extra nutrition, the extra nourishment they need, by making them naturally aggressive. *Watch out for those little ones.* I quickly filed that advice under Ignore. Now I'm no longer ignoring that advice. What I'm thinking is, *Woo*, and wishing I had a couple of nurses here to offer advice or spell me for a bit, because I'm actually tired, physically *tired*, as if from a workout, by this effort of watching my daughter.

I know just how it feels to arrive at an understanding too late. Here, on the sixth day in, I realize that this problem has a strangely symmetrical solution. I've been hoping to have victory on my terms—she stays put in there, and I remain out here, with my drink, my book, and my freedom. But the impulse that nature has given my daughter for her own protection—this aggressive nature that tells her to go after the food she needs, to go out and get things and *survive*—doesn't have an off switch. The role of thwarter and boundary setter is not a role I want, but I will play it—though I won't be playing it from a distance. This is how things have to be— she was born light and is who she is. So I change the rules of the game, in a way that allows both of us a small victory: I set aside my drink and book and climb inside the little minimum-security prison with her, where I will remain until it's time to go.

Rosemary-Smoked Steak
Serves 2

Note that the steak wears its chopped-rosemary rub for an hour—the salt in the rub causes the steak's juices to move to the surface, where the rosemary flavor hitches a ride before the juices are drawn back inside. The recipe builds on an extra note of flavor by adding some rosemary smoke to the mix.

For a nice accompaniment, try Grilled Radicchio with "Broken" Roasted Garlic Vinaigrette (page 167).

> 1 teaspoon finely minced fresh rosemary
>
> 1 teaspoon kosher salt
>
> ½ teaspoon freshly ground black pepper
>
> 1 rib-eye, boneless shell, or porterhouse steak (about 1½ pounds), 1½ inches thick
>
> 1 teaspoon olive oil
>
> 6 sprigs fresh rosemary, each about the size of your index finger

SPECIAL EQUIPMENT

Meat thermometer

1. One hour before you're ready to grill the steak, combine the rosemary, salt, and pepper. Lay the steak on the counter and rub all surfaces with the rosemary mixture, then wrap tightly in plastic wrap. Set the wrapped steak on a plate and leave the plate on the counter, out of the refrigerator, for 1 hour.

2. When the steak has rested for nearly an hour, preheat your grill to the highest heat possible, whether using briquettes or a gas grill. You're ready to grill when you can hold your hand a few inches over the grill for just a second or two.

3. Unwrap the steak and use a paper towel to pat the steak dry. Rub the steak with the oil. Quickly wet the rosemary sprigs, then shake off all excess water—you want them to be just barely damp. Lay the steak on the grill, then push half the rosemary sprigs through the grates, directly onto the heat source, as close as possible to the steak. Close the grill cover and grill 3 minutes, undisturbed. Lift the cover, flip the steak, push the remaining rosemary sprigs through the grates, and cover the grill again. Grill 3 minutes undisturbed, then move the steak to a platter and take the temperature of the exact center with a meat thermometer—you want the steak to be about 125°F for medium rare. Depending on the heat of your grill, you may be there, or you may need another minute or two. Continue to grill, turning once or twice, until the center registers 125°F for a perfectly cooked medium-rare steak, 8 to 10 minutes total.

4. When the steak reaches the desired doneness, allow it to rest, uncovered, on the platter for 5 minutes so the juices can redistribute, and serve.

Grilled Radicchio with "Broken" Roasted Garlic Vinaigrette

Serves 4 (as appetizers)

I love bitter flavors. Many other people love bitter flavors too—but most like just a hint of it, not an overwhelming amount. Here I've taken a bitter ingredient (grilled radicchio) and balanced it with the natural sweetness of roasted garlic and balsamic vinegar—in fact, I intentionally leave the vinaigrette only partially emulsified, so that on the plate you get naked bits of roasted garlic and vinegar that offer up fresh hits of sweetness.

> 1 whole garlic head, top ¼ inch sliced off so the tops of some cloves are exposed
>
> ½ cup plus 3 tablespoons olive oil
>
> 2½ tablespoons best-quality balsamic vinegar, preferably aged
>
> ½ tablespoon Dijon mustard
>
> ½ teaspoon salt, plus more for seasoning
>
> Freshly ground black pepper, to taste
>
> 1 teaspoon minced fresh rosemary
>
> 1 large head radicchio, quartered from root end so that quarters stay intact
>
> 4 sprigs fresh rosemary, for garnish

1. Preheat the oven to 375°F.

2. Rub the head of garlic all over with 1 tablespoon of the oil, then wrap loosely in a layer of foil and bake for 1 hour, until soft. Remove head of garlic from foil and set aside to cool. When garlic has cooled, pull the roasted garlic cloves out of their paper skins, and discard the skins and garlic shell. Mash the garlic cloves to a paste with a fork.

3. Add 2½ tablespoons of the mashed roasted garlic to a Tupperware container or a jar with a lid. Add the balsamic vinegar, mustard, salt, pepper, and minced rosemary, cover tightly, and shake well. Uncover, add ½ cup of the oil, cover again, and shake well until the vinaigrette is partially emulsified. Set aside.

4. Preheat a grill to the highest heat possible, whether using briquettes or a gas grill. Rub the radicchio quarters with the remaining 2 tablespoons olive oil, then grill, turning occasionally, until nicely browned and beginning to slightly fan out, about 5 minutes total. Remove to a plate and season well with salt and pepper.

5. Set out 4 small plates, and place one of the grilled radicchio quarters in the center of each plate. Shake the roasted garlic vinai-

grette lightly once more, then uncover and spoon a thin line of the vinaigrette around the perimeter of each plate. Spoon some of the vinaigrette over the radicchio quarters too. With any luck, the vinaigrette will be imperfectly emulsified, and there will be bits of garlic and pure vinegar hiding amid a slick of olive oil. (You'll have more vinaigrette than you need—save the remaining vinaigrette for another use, such as a salad dressing or marinade for chicken.) Garnish each plate with a rosemary sprig and serve.

Red Snapper with Ginger-Scallion Oil

Serves 2 adults and 1 child

During vacations I like to stand outside barefoot while making dinner, so I grill even when I'm pan-searing. An iron skillet can certainly handle the heat. And this approach comes with a clear benefit: Using the grill instead of the stove when cooking fish means your kitchen won't have fish odors the next day.

The ginger-scallion rice recipe (page 31) minus the fried egg, would be a good accompaniment for this.

FOR THE GINGER-SCALLION OIL

½ cup peanut, grapeseed, or other neutral oil

2 scallions, green and white parts, coarsely chopped

2 tablespoons peeled and coarsely chopped fresh ginger

FOR THE FISH

2 red snapper fillets, skin-on (about 8 ounces each)

Salt and freshly ground black pepper

4 scallions (white and pale green parts only), julienned

Note: Before serving this to a child, be sure she has first eaten flaky white fish with no allergic reaction.

1. *Make the ginger-scallion oil:* Add the oil, scallions, and ginger to a food processor or blender and coarsely puree. Pour into a bowl and allow to rest for 20 minutes, then strain and discard solids. Set oil aside.

2. *Sear the fish:* Preheat the grill to its hottest temperature. While the grill is heating up, lay the frying pan directly on the grate so it will preheat too.

3. Score the fish fillets on the skin side and season very well with salt and pepper. Carry a tray with a clean plate, the fish fillets, and 3 tablespoons of the ginger-scallion oil out to the grill. (Reserve the rest of the ginger-scallion oil for plating in step 4.) Add the 3 tablespoons oil to the cast-iron skillet. When the oil just begins to smoke, slide the snapper fillets into the skillet and close the lid of the grill. Allow the snapper fillets to roast 4 minutes, then flip (if the fillets stick, use a metal spatula to carefully scrape the fillets up off the skillet) and roast about 3 minutes, until browned on both sides and just cooked through. Lay the fillets skin side up on the clean plate to rest, and bring them inside.

4. To serve, divide the snapper fillets, skin side up, onto two plates. Spoon a thin line of ginger-scallion oil around the perimeter of each plate, and top each plate with a generous pinch of julienned scallions. Serve immediately—watch out for pinbones in the fish. If you want to serve the fish to a child, I recommend that you pick through the fish first and discard any bones you find. (Leftover ginger-scallion oil can be stored in the refrigerator for a few days—it may set up; just bring it back to room temperature to use it.)

american nightmare

We're in Stamford on a slightly chilly, sunny afternoon, here to meet Jessica's mother for lunch.

Signs of the times are all around us.

First, in the park before lunch—Gracie is laboriously pushing, pushing, pushing a stroller around a block-sized park just outside the center of town. Lovely grass; quiet setting. We're a bit early for lunch and are burning the clock with time on the lawn. Pushing the stroller is hard work on the damp sod, still treacherous with yesterday's rain, but Gracie seems to enjoy it, and she certainly doesn't want me offering any help or, at least, any help that she's aware she's being given. Still, I'm tailing her at a slight distance, for three reasons:

The first reason is that she's wearing a white sweater that will cease to be a white sweater the instant she falls down.

The second reason is that every so often the stroller hits a slick patch of grass and begins to roll much more quickly than it has been, which means that a quick-strike grab of the stroller frame is the only thing preventing her from going face first into the stroller basket.

The third reason I'm trailing her—the first sign of the times—is the Wasted Man.

He wasn't here when we arrived.

He just showed up somehow while we weren't looking.

I think what frightens me most about the Wasted Man is that he's dressed fairly respectably, in clean clothes. He has a nice haircut, new shoes, good teeth, clean fingernails, and he's stinking drunk. Drunk to the point that he can't stand well, so he decides, a few moments after he arrives, to lie down bodily on the wet ground, his weaving head propped up on one fist, his elbow's already questionable support looking like it might give out at any moment. He's watching Gracie with eyes gone glossy with sentimental tears; one can only guess that his mind's eye is torturing him with images of a child of his own. Does he have horrible news to deliver to his family? Or did he just *receive* horrible news from his family? I sense that I would, for reasons that aren't entirely clear to me, feel somewhat less uneasy if he were obviously a lifelong thief, sick on junk, insane. But no, this man seems more like a near-picture of suburban propriety who walked out his front door, planning to have a perfectly ordinary day—and had a piano dropped on his head. Did he lose his job? That seems the likely answer, in these times when that's true of one out of every ten persons out there. A decisive piece of bad luck has driven him to this lowly state. In other words, this man is not the Other you spy in the crack dealer, the hustler, the cheat down the corner, the person separated from you by so many factors. No, this man here with us is You; he is Me.

Which is another way of saying he could be any one of us.

This could happen to me if I lose my job.

I've had much good fortune in this life. Quality health care, an excellent education, frequent dental care, a good career, a loving family, opportunity, opportunity, opportunity. A life that is sometimes labeled, particularly by those who have traveled here from another country seeking a better life, the American dream. But in these times—admit it—we're all just one pink slip away from a terrible American Nightmare: the dream turned inside out, and shorn of its self-sustaining dignity.

Helicopter dad. That's me.

Because men like this one are everywhere these days, a sign of the times.

A little bit later. At the restaurant.

We're outside, sitting at a scrolled-iron table with Jessica's mother. Enjoying the sunny weather, the way the light has retained its force, and summer seems to be hanging on despite the chill. A pleasant row of tables lines the walk beneath the restaurant's awning. Ambient air is doing a good job of maintaining my untouched Guiness's temperature as I trail Gracie around patio, over curb, through hedge—she's become obsessed with circling through the loose grouping of bushes that divides the restaurant tables from the sidewalk. I could just let her walk, right? Let her travel where she likes and observe from a distance. Let her range without me hanging all over her and stop being such a helicopter dad, the kind people make fun of, that's me, and I hate that about myself and want to stop but my mind is still on the Wasted Man and that look he gave her. It carried a vibration of such certain doom, and a lucidity bordering on madness, that I would have been entirely unsurprised to trail Grace through the hedge and find her, on the far side, transfixed on the sidewalk, staring up at the Wasted Man with her mouth gone into an *O* of shock, the tears in her eyes reflecting the tears in his. Would he take her hand? Seize her in a hug?

Snatch her up and run?

His apparent lurch from the mundane into the berserk tells a story of a man who has lost everything. Which is another way of saying that anything, from this point forward, is allowed.

Our lunch ends with another sign of the times.

I follow Gracie through the hedge one last time. This is it, baby girl, then I'm going back to my Guinness and I'm going to stop thinking about that poor bastard. Because he put the whammy on me, this guy. How difficult is it to fall that hard? Not that difficult. Not that difficult at all, when the market keeps doing its subtraction thing. Which is the only thing it seems to be doing, lately.

She has a new word, Grace. Lately, when she notices something that apprehends her interest, she stops walking, squats down before the object, points to it, and simultaneously looks back at me and asks, Ih? (= *what is this?*)

Our last trip through the hedge ends with one of these moments. I'm five feet behind Gracie, and on her way through to the sidewalk, she stops.

Squats. Points and turns to look back at me.

"Ih?" she asks.

What is this?

I creep up on her and peer over her shoulder.

An assortment of festively colored plastic pieces. Scattered on the ground I see red, orange, yellow, green, blue, indigo, violet. They look like pieces of candy or at least as if they should be used to transport little bits of candy—something nice and sweet.

It takes me a moment—then I notice the plastic tubes they're attached to, and the dime drops.

Ih?

Crack vials, Grace. Those are crack vials, a sign of the times. And we're leaving.

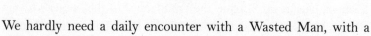

We hardly need a daily encounter with a Wasted Man, with a cache of spent crack vials, to know that lives everywhere are being ruined. The evidence is on display in the foreclosure signs we pass whenever we drive *anywhere*, through wealthy and poor neighborhoods alike. Jessica and I sometimes try to count them, to see how many we can tally along the lonely lane we're driving, and what begins as a macabre game quickly evolves into an astonished tally that leaves us sick for the families at risk of losing everything. *This is You; This is Me.* The evidence is there when the news comes over the phone that yet another good, kind, capable friend has, through no fault of her own, lost her job and her livelihood— should you call immediately and offer empathy? Does she want to be left alone? Does she want to break something, scream? *This is You; this is Me.* The evidence is there when Jessica tells me about friends who have cut spending to the bone, introduced family budgets, sold prized possessions. *This is You; this is Me.*

In fact, this is us. Jessica and I sit at the kitchen table—not across from each other but side by side, because we refuse to be anything but absolutely together in this—and we try to figure it out. We have a problem. When the market crashed, it took with it vast sums of the money we had saved and invested; much worse, it also placed the newspaper industry, already wrestling with the advent of Internet-distributed news, in a risky state of transition. We're committed to many, many more months of our lease; should I lose my job, the rent alone would devastate what we've worked to build. And somehow, with less and less money coming in, all our bills seem to be going *up.* Corporations are all but billing me for the paper the bill is printed on, the ink used to display the font, the water for the coffeepot. Familiar with this? That sense of freefall you experience when you wrench open that Old Testament of bills and stare at the rising numbers, wondering if perhaps they've been translated into rubles or marks or even lira? But no, those are American dollars, and contemplating them inspires me to reflect on the modern condition: a state in which the absolute basics of rent, heat, food, and transportation take every dollar you make and then some.

At night, the windows of the surrounding apartments invariably frame men pacing anxiously within their bright lairs. Why is it always men I encounter at night, as if it's only women who have the sense to get to bed and figure things out in the morning? It occurs to me that these men are doing exactly what I am—*they're* watching *me.* I study these Others, these double-walkers, with great interest, each so close I could drain the highball in his hand with a single shot of a BB gun—but we're no better off for having recognized each other and achieved a sort of gloomy solidarity. This doesn't help, the understanding that *we're all in this together.* I should, after all, be surrounded by people who know better. I know that I don't know better, because I have no investing acumen whatsoever. I buy a stock, and the next day the fever line charting its value does its impression of a winged bird, and I learn that every forecaster out there *knew* this was going to happen. I put a bid on an apartment, a piece of real estate I'm positive is a good buy—and the next day learn that the building next door is about to be razed. As with the dud stock I bought, I soon discover that these are things everyone with half a brain already knew and took as a sign to stay away. I missed the Internet boom. And I missed the real estate boom. Whatever the next boom is, you can rest assured I'll miss that one too. There's a decent chance that this next boom is already here and I just don't know about it.

The mathematics, anyway, suggest the boom has gone away and has been replaced by a bust. My 401(k) falls off a cliff and threatens to become worth less than the amount I have contributed. Up ahead is the exquisite pain of salary givebacks. The fact that my investments turn to shit is hardly surprising—that's what always happens. But now they turn to shit *faster.* Gracie is walking now and needs new shoes; she's outgrown the pair we just bought her. *Don't complain, idiot—not so long ago you wanted nothing but for her to grow.* I'm steadily finding out what it's like to work twice as hard yet move backward in time—see the money I have worked to earn evaporate. In short: I experience exactly what's happening to everyone else out there.

We sit at the table and add it up, and we quickly get it: After the obvious costs of rent and transportation, food is the clear leader in our living expenses. So the red pen flashes from its scabbard, and Jessica and I slice and dice that grocery bill with the ruthless skill of sushi chefs. We've long since traded top-shelf meats and fish and shellfish for less-exalted cuts and species that require more care for less cost. Beef tenderloin is out; pork tenderloin is in. Good-bye, sole; hello, tilapia, nice to meet you. No more duck confit; lots more chicken leg. We use out-of-the-ordinary ingredients (garlic confit, roasted artichokes, poached eggs, legume-based stews) as centerpieces and make maximum use of Italian starches (polenta, hand-cut sheets of fresh pasta) that we've spiked with flashy sauces (like one I devised from the juice of roasted red peppers). We punch up soups with wine and dried mushrooms. We make our own version of staple items we used to buy—chicken stock, simple pickles, bread crumbs ginned up out of stale bread. It's not enough, though—it's never enough. You know how it is. Save fifty bucks, and you find yourself wishing you'd saved sixty. Save sixty, and you wish you'd reached for a hundred. Every future tuition bill looms like a glittering sword of Damocles; I cringe when I think of the bill for my daughter's wedding, not because I won't be thrilled to pay it, but because *I'm afraid I won't have the money.*

Fear is, of course, at the heart of it all. In those rare moments when I'm being entirely honest with myself, I realize that I'm afraid I won't be able to provide for my daughter the life that my parents provided for me, which means I will have somehow failed in my task to make good on those gifts. How lucky it is, then, that I have been given a gift from the opposite end of my history: the fear of disappointing my child. Were I ever to lose my job, I'd never, ever, end up like that man we encountered in the park. The loss of a means of providing for my child would not send me over that particular set of falls. It's not that I don't have the seed of such a surrender lurking in me. It's just that I could never bear to have Gracie see me in such a state.

In this way also, Gracie is both the problem and the solution.

Focaccia al Formaggio

Serves 2

One of the finest representations of *cucina povera*, the recipe was supposedly developed hundreds of years ago, when the people of and around Genoa, Italy, found themselves under regular attack by the Saracen raiders. To escape these raids, they would take cover in the mountains, where they were forced to cook with the bare minimum of durable ingredients at hand—flour, olive oil, salt, local cheeses, and perhaps some wild herbs, all of it mixed together with water from a nearby stream.

FOR THE DOUGH

2 cups all-purpose flour

¾ cup minus 1 tablespoon water

2 tablespoons extra virgin olive oil

½ teaspoon salt

FOR THE FOCACCIA

4 teaspoons extra virgin olive oil

½ pound fresh mozzarella cheese—gently squeeze the mozzarella in a paper towel to remove excess moisture

¼ cup freshly grated pecorino cheese

½ teaspoon finely chopped fresh rosemary

SPECIAL EQUIPMENT

14-inch rimmed round baking sheet—a standard pizza baking sheet, really, but make sure it has a raised rim

1. Place an oven rack in the middle of the oven and preheat the oven to 500°F for at least 30 minutes.

2. *Make the dough:* Combine the flour, water, oil, and salt in a food

processor fitted with the dough blade and start the machine. The dough will take about 15 seconds to come together into a ball—after it comes together, continue to process for about 45 seconds. Turn off the machine and allow the dough to rest for 15 minutes.

3. *Make the focaccia:* Move the dough to a well-floured work surface and shape into a ball. Divide into 2 equal pieces, and shape each into a ball. Roll out the first ball very, very thinly—you'll want to use plenty of flour on both sides of the sheet you're rolling out, as this will help it roll easily. If you've rolled it out correctly, you'll have a dough circle about 16 inches in diameter (or, preferably, slightly more) when you're through.

4. Pour 2 teaspoons of the oil into the rimmed baking sheet and rub the oil over the entire surface, including the rim, using your hands. Lay the dough sheet you just rolled out over the baking sheet—there should be a little extra dough hanging over the edge. Feel free to stretch it a bit to get some overhang. Press the dough down so that it conforms to the sheet.

5. Tear the fresh mozzarella into 1-inch pieces and dot the cheese evenly over the entire sheet of dough. Sprinkle with the pecorino cheese, then rosemary. Drizzle 1 teaspoon olive oil over the cheese and herbs.

6. Roll out the second ball of dough the same way you rolled out the first—again, you want at least a 16-inch sheet of dough. Stretch the sheet over the top of the pan to form a top layer over the cheese. Press the tines of a fork around the entire perimeter of the focaccia to make the top and bottom edges stick together, then use scissors to trim away the extra dough extending beyond the rim of the baking sheet. Make six 1-inch tears around the surface of the focaccia to allow steam to escape and the cheese to peek through.

7. Drizzle the top of the dough with the remaining teaspoon of oil, then sprinkle with coarse salt. Slide in the oven. Bake for 5 minutes, then spin the baking sheet. Bake for about 6 minutes more, until the focaccia is well browned in spots and crispy, with little tiny bubbles raised here and there on the surface. Serve immediately.

Cappellini with Red Pepper "Water" and Rosemary

Serves 2 to 3

Serve with some bread, scavenge a few ingredients from your refrigerator, and it'll easily feed four people for less than ten dollars.

> 5 whole red peppers
>
> 2 thick slices stale or fresh sourdough or other artisanal bread
>
> 5 tablespoons olive oil
>
> ½ medium Spanish onion, diced
>
> ½ cup dry white wine
>
> Salt
>
> ½ pound dried angel hair pasta
>
> 2 teaspoons minced fresh rosemary
>
> ¼ cup freshly grated Parmesan cheese
>
> Freshly ground black pepper
>
> 2 teaspoons finely chopped fresh parsley

1. Place a large pot of salted water to boil over high heat. Place an oven rack as close to the broiler as possible and preheat the broiler. Broil the peppers, turning occasionally (very gently, being careful not to break them open), until charred all over, 10 to 15 minutes.

2. Place the peppers in a bowl and cover tightly with plastic wrap or foil. Allow the peppers to cool for 20 minutes, then remove the cover, and, one at a time, working entirely over the bowl, gently crack open each pepper and let all the juice drain out of the peppers into the bowl in which they've been resting. Discard as many seeds as you can, then peel and discard the charred skins and pepper stems. Set the flesh of the roasted peppers aside as you finish peeling them. Strain the juice you collected in the bowl to get rid of all seeds—your ultimate goal is a small

bowl of seedless red pepper juice, with any luck somewhere around ¾ cup to 1 cup. (Dress the roasted red peppers you've set aside with a little olive oil, place in a bowl, cover, refrigerate, and save for another use.)

3. Toast the bread slices briefly to dry them, then add the bread to a food processor or blender. Blend until crumbs the texture of coarse soil form. Heat 2 tablespoons of the oil in a large skillet over medium-high heat. When the oil shimmers, add the bread crumbs. Toast the bread crumbs, stirring and tossing frequently, until browned and nicely crisped, about 4 minutes. Pour the bread crumbs into a bowl and set aside.

4. Heat the remaining 3 tablespoons of oil in a large skillet over medium-high heat. Add the onion and sauté, stirring often, until soft, about 3 minutes. Add the wine to the onion, raise the heat, and bring to a boil; then lower the heat and simmer.

5. While you're bringing the wine to a simmer, add the pasta to the boiling water and cook according to the directions on the box. When the pasta is almost ready, reserve ¼ cup of the pasta water. Drain the pasta and add to the simmering wine in the skillet. Add the red pepper water you collected in the bowl, the rosemary, reserved pasta water, and cheese. Season with salt and pepper and stir to combine well. Allow the pasta to simmer in the sauce, stirring occasionally, for another minute, then plate, drizzling any extra sauce around the plates. Scatter the chopped parsley over the pasta and serve. Pass the bowl of crispy bread crumbs at the table.

Leek, Mushroom, and Thyme Tart

Serves 4

A recipe that makes the humble, sublime, yet amazingly inexpensive leek the star of the show. It is a fair amount of work, so save this one for a long, leisurely weekend afternoon.

2 tablespoons olive oil

2 cups mushrooms, preferably cremini, sliced

3 tablespoons unsalted butter

5 sprigs fresh thyme

6 to 8 large leeks (white and pale green parts only), washed well and sliced thinly

4 large shallots, peeled and sliced thinly

4 garlic cloves, sliced thinly

½ Spanish onion, sliced thinly

Small bunch of chives, sliced into ½-inch lengths

Salt and freshly ground black pepper

1 cup heavy cream (don't substitute light cream or half and half)

1 prebaked Savory Pastry Shell (page 183)

1. Preheat the oven to 400°F.

2. Heat the oil over medium-high heat in a wide skillet. When the oil is very hot, add the mushrooms and sauté until they throw off their water and begin to brown, 6 to 8 minutes. Add 1 tablespoon of the butter and 1 sprig of thyme and sauté an additional minute, then pour the mushrooms into a bowl and wipe out the skillet with a paper towel. In the same skillet, heat the remaining 2 tablespoons of butter over medium heat and add the leeks, shallots, garlic, and onion and sauté until soft and translucent but not at all browned, about 5 minutes. Add the chives and combine well. Season with salt and pepper. Remove the skillet from the heat.

3. Add the cream to a small saucepan. Bring the cream to a low boil over medium-high heat, and boil gently for 15 to 20 minutes until reduced to ½ cup. (Watch the cream closely as it boils to make sure it doesn't boil over.) *Very important:* After you've boiled the cream down, pour it into a measuring cup to be sure you've reduced it to ½ cup. If you don't reduce the cream enough, the finished tart will be a watery mess.

4. Pour the leek mixture into the savory pastry shell. (Don't press it down—let it lay loosely in the shell.) Pour the cream over the leeks. Scatter the mushrooms over the surface, then arrange the remaining 4 sprigs of thyme on the surface in a pattern. Bake until firm, about 30 minutes. Allow the tart to cool and set for at least 5 minutes before slicing. Can be served at any temperature.

Savory Pastry Shell

Makes one 9-inch pie shell

1½ cups all-purpose flour

Pinch of salt

8 tablespoons unsalted butter, chilled and cut into small cubes, plus 1 tablespoon, at room temperature, for greasing the pan

4 tablespoons very cold water

1. Put the flour, salt, and the 8 chilled and cubed tablespoons of butter in a food processor fitted with the dough blade and pulse until what's in the bowl resembles coarse crumbs, about 8 pulses. Add the water and pulse about 6 or 7 more times until the dough just barely begins to come together. (You may need to add an additional table-spoon of water to convince the dough to barely come together.) Turn the dough out of the bowl onto a piece of plastic wrap or parchment paper. Shape into a ball, wrap tightly, then flatten the dough into an even disc. Place in the refrigerator for ½ hour.

2. While the dough rests, preheat the oven to 350°F.

3. Grease a 9-inch tart pan or pie dish with the remaining table-spoon butter. After the dough has chilled, transfer it to a lightly floured work surface and roll it out, adding additional flour occasion-

ally so it doesn't stick to the surface or the rolling pin, until it's large enough to fill the tart pan or pie dish with a little overlap.

4. To transfer the dough to the pan or dish, loosen the far edge and the roll it back over your rolling pin—then drape the dough into the pan or dish. (Did the dough tear? Don't worry—just use an extra scrap of dough to patch the tear.) Press down gently into the corners of the dish or pan. Prick the dough with a fork, then cover with foil and fill the foil with dried beans or uncooked rice (the beans or rice will weigh the dough down as it prebakes). Bake the dough this way for 20 minutes, then remove the foil and the beans or rice and bake 10 more minutes. Set aside to cool.

a moment of clarity

With the dreadful financial news quickening, I find myself arriving home after work thirsty for something with more kick than a mere glass of water. I don't want a cocktail—I want four of them. Which is another way of saying that the last thing I need is a cocktail. But my blood wants one and won't shut up about it.

Though New York outside is mired in forbidding November, I'm vacationing in a balmy and temperate place I call Delusion, and here in Delusion, a sort of Las Vegas of the mind, you are tempted to drink a lot. I hide in Delusion because when I'm *not* there, the questions are just too frightening to face. *Are you meeting your bills?* Barely. *Are you saving any money?* No. *Are you losing money?* Absolutely. *When will we see the third book?* I don't know. *How's is it coming along?* Poorly, if at all. The thing I rely on to keep me from going nuts has abandoned me. Nothing good can come of this, this practice of relying on alcohol to provide that warm, contented glow that will get me through the evening without suffering a case of the cold sweats. Nothing good can come of this, especially when you have kids.

Half past six. I let myself in the front door, drop my bag and coat, and then watch, with a mixture of amusement and fear, as Gracie picks up my bag and coat and pretends to put them on, pretends that she's getting ready to go off to work—in short, pretends that *she is me*. My habits are becoming her habits, which suggests that my relationship with alcohol will, someday, become *her* relationship with alcohol—and this means moderation, moderation, moderation. Beer or a simple glass of wine are on offer, of course, but those don't scratch the itch the way a shaken drink does, even one that's had its effects carefully tamped down. I've always been interested in dreaming up new drinks, but now, with this little mime tottering around the apartment dragging my coat and bag behind her, watching my every move, I realize that I must do so determined to hit a special mark: to make cocktails that are no stronger than a standard glass of wine.

First I try pairing small amounts of vodka, gin, and bourbon with greater amounts of fruit juice, fruit purees, or sparkling waters, but the results are disappointing, resembling watered-down versions of standard cocktails and sometimes tasting decidedly dull. I have better luck when I switch to making drinks composed almost entirely of fortified wines, sparkling wines, and liqueurs. The list of aperitifs one can choose from is nearly endless, as just about every region around the world has its own local specialty: Lillet from Bordeaux, sherry from Cádiz, Campari from Milan. The bottles are gleaming and candy-colored, so fetching they cause Gracie to drop my coat and bag and come investigate what Dad is doing.

"Gracie," I say, "I'm having a drink, but I'm maintaining. I'm following the rule book on responsible-dad protocol."

"Eye!" Gracie says.

"Hi back," I say.

Back to work, with my kid watching me. Lillet, sweet vermouth, dry vermouth, crème de cassis, fresh lime juice, and orange liqueur deliver so many competing flavors and textures—sweet, velvety, sharp, fruity, citrusy, bitter, and flinty—I'm overwhelmed by a single sip and pour the rest down the drain. A much pared-down effort that follows has half as many ingredients—Lillet, freshly

squeezed orange juice, and a splash of Campari—and is as refreshing a drink as any on memory. The first sip transforms me
into an optimist. My high hopes for the addition of effervescent
waters like Pellegrino, though, are misguided: Because milder
drinks are already noticeably lighter than traditional cocktails,
dilution with sparkling water makes them taste like something
one should drink over ice rather than shaken and poured into a
chilled cocktail glass. Forget effervescent waters, I think. Try effervescent wines instead. Try *frizzante*. And here we have a clear
success: Cava plus sherry plus sweet vermouth with lemon peel.
Simplicity itself, and now my little warm optimistic glow is expanding.

"Gracie," I say. "What shall we call it?"

Every respectable cocktail, after all, requires a name. I'm usually unable to think of something clever, though, so most of the
time I just name a new drink after something that's going on
in my life at the time. Littered throughout my drink-concocting
history are literal-minded winners like the Boat Won't Start
(invented two summers ago, after I found myself adrift one afternoon in the middle of Lake Winnipesaukee) and the Smit-
ten Kitten (developed after I got some inside information about
how my then future wife felt our first date had gone). As I sip
my drink, thinking over different possible names, I recall a brief
period of madness that took hold when Gracie began sleeping through the night. Convinced that we'd all sleep fine in a
fifteen-by-fifteen-foot hotel room, I asked Jessica if we should
take a family vacation in Spain.

"The Barcelona Delusion, Gracie," I say, and it fits.

I decide that I like a good Delusion, and will have another.

Eye! Gracie says. *Ih?* she asks, and says, *Eh.*

I know what she means.

She can really talk, this kid of mine, not just with the halting words but with the sign language that Jessica has taught her. When I ask her, Gracie, are you all done with your dinner or would you like some more? she says, *Muh, muh,* and taps the fingertips of her right and left hands together (= *more*).

Later, I ask her, Gracie are you all done with your dinner or would you like some more?

Deh, deh, she says, moving her open hands side to side at her waist (= *done*).

I ask her, Gracie, do you want juice or milk?

Meh, she says, and bends the fingers of one hand to pat the tips to her palm (= *milk*).

I ask her, Gracie, do you want to climb the steps or go inside? *Dih,* she says (= *steps*).

I ask her, Gracie, do you want to read books or take a bath?

She opens and closes her fist above her head (= *shower* = *bath*).

I ask her, Gracie, you look tired—is it time for your nap?

She presses her open palm to the side of her face (= *night, night*).

Night, night. I've learned that as a parent you never fully shut down. Even when I'm deeply asleep, one vital component of my consciousness is awake, listening at the night as closely as the most delicate seismograph, seeking any sounds of infant distress. The words my daughter has spoken during the day always seem to resonate in the nighttime inner ear. There in my sleep I hear an ambient *Ih?* and *deh* and *dih* and other words—but what I hear most is *Eye!*

In my sleep, Gracie is always saying *Eye!* and I'm always saying, *Hi back.*

The Delusion's awfully good. But it comes with a terrible hangover.

Later that night, I watch Gracie pull books down from the shelf.

Woo, I think, *watch out for those little ones.* Paperback, hardback, paperback, hardback—now it's a rainfall of words and pages, and it will be left to me to put those stories back later. Gracie brings them down rapid-fire, then tramps round on them, or picks them up and drops them from a great height. Books are fun for Gracie, though for the time being they are, understandably, more cherished for their structural services than for their content.

Now she pulls down my copy of *Where I'm Calling From*—and then, instead of moving on to the next book, pauses, crouches down, and studies the cover photograph of Raymond Carver's face. Now here is some content that has grabbed her attention.

"Dada," she says, tapping his face.

Dada writes books, yes.

"Dada, dada," she says.

Where I'm Calling From was the first book I ever loved as a writer rather than as a reader, a good luck charm that I read over and over, mining the pages for evidence that would inform on the nature of literary success—though the cover photograph itself supplied much of what I needed to know. Carver's face, in the photograph, is lined with experience, and pain, and other things.

She taps his face again and looks up at me.

"Dada," she says. "Dada."

Dada writes books, yes. But not lately. Lately he's become a little bit lost.

I turn and walk into the kitchen, feeling, strangely, as if I'm being *propelled* by something—another of those unexpected thunderbolts of understanding, I suppose, though I haven't fully decoded its message.

A bowl of Macoun apples, left over from an apple-picking trip we took a few weeks ago, rests on the counter. I pick one up and hold it in my hand, surprised by its compact weight. We arrived that afternoon wondering how well Gracie would take to it, if the trees and abundance and activity would somehow seem overwhelming, but we hadn't got twenty feet into the orchard before she made it apparent that she wanted an apple for herself, point-

ing and calling for me to pull one down for her. I twisted the
nearest Macoun off the branch, then realized that I couldn't give
it to her with the peel on—it was too tough for her young teeth,
too tannic. I had no peeler handy, though, so I did what I'd been
doing every day and night for the past year: I improvised. With
my incisors I carved the peel off the apple, filling my mouth with
the bitter taste, and then handed her the first whole apple she'd
ever have, a gift of sweetness I never expected to get back—and
was at once devastated yet totally unsurprised when, after turning the apple over in her little fists, she squinted up at me and
held the apple out, offering me the first bite.

Is this the way out of the motionless stall I find myself in, not
through the writing of an *Error*, a record of paranoia, but through
the writing of a record of a regeneration of faith, in which the
problem and solution are one?

I watch my daughter bring more books down off the shelf,
and that seismograph I use to listen at the night gives a sudden
shiver, as if Gracie has just shouted *Eye!*

And I think, *Hi back.*

Pan-Roasted Sweet Apple Sandwich
with Bourbon Butter

Serves 2

After you make this dessert for the first time, you'll realize what it is: an
analog of a grilled cheese sandwich. I devised it after messing around
with a complicated apple tart recipe for a while and deciding that it

was just plain wrong to offer two very difficult pastry recipes in one book. Instead, what you have here is a simple, sweet, crispy sandwich filled with pristine apple slices.

> 2 tablespoons unsalted butter, softened to room temperature
>
> 1½ teaspoons bourbon or brandy
>
> 1 teaspoon honey
>
> 1 large sweet apple, such a Macoun or Gala
>
> 4 thick slices sourdough or other artisanal white bread

1. In a small bowl, mash together the butter, bourbon, and honey with a fork or spatula until completely combined.

2. Spread the bourbon butter on all slices of bread—on *both* sides. Use all of the butter. (You cover all surfaces because you don't just want the butter on the surface of the sandwiches, you want it inside too.)

3. Peel and core the apple, then slice into thin slices. Lay two of the bread slices on a cutting board or plate, top each with half the sliced apples, then top each with another slice of bread—creating two apple sandwiches.

4. Lay the sandwiches in a cold skillet, and place the skillet over medium heat. After 4 to 5 minutes, when the sandwiches come to a good strong sizzle, use a knife to gently lift and peek beneath—the sugars in the butter will cause the bread to brown much more quickly than it would with a grilled cheese, so it's best to begin checking early. (The pan will also smoke more easily than usual.) When the sandwiches are very dark brown underneath, carefully flip them. Because there isn't any cheese to hold this grilled sandwich together, I find it's best to press down on the top of the sandwich with one hand while sliding a spatula beneath the sandwich—then flip the sandwich while continuing to hold the sandwich together between your hand and the spatula.

5. Brown on the second side—again, after 3 to 4 minutes, peek beneath by lifting with a knife. When the second side is very well browned, slide the sandwich onto a plate and serve.

The Bitter Heiress

This drink looks awfully swanky in the glass, and the flaming process is quite a show for those who have never seen it before. I would, however, recommend practicing flaming a citrus peel a few times before you try it in front of others.

> 3 ounces Lillet
>
> 1 ounce freshly squeezed orange juice
>
> 1 good splash Campari
>
> 1 thick, oval lemon peel or orange peel, about 2 inches in diameter
>
> 1 orange peel, for garnish

Note: Total alcohol = about .55 ounces, depending on amount of Campari used

Fill a cocktail shaker with ice. Add the Lillet, orange juice, and Campari. Stir rapidly with a knife or bar spoon until the outside of the shaker is frosted, then strain into a chilled martini glass. Hold the oval peel by the edges between your thumb and forefinger, with the peel facing the drink, about 3 inches above the surface of the drink. Strike a match with the other hand and hold between the peel and the drink. Squeeze the peel sharply so it bends toward the match to flame the citrus oil and spray it onto the surface of the drink. Discard match and squeezed peel. Garnish the drink with the remaining orange peel and serve.

The Barcelona Delusion

This one's pure candy for people who prefer their alcohol *frizzante*.

    1 ounce dry Spanish sherry, such as fino, amontillado, or
       oloroso
    1 ounce sweet vermouth
    2 ounces ice-cold Cava or dry champagne or Prosecco
    1 lemon peel

Note: Total alcohol = .58 ounces

Fill a cocktail shaker with ice. Add the sherry and vermouth. Stir rapidly with a knife or bar spoon until the outside of the shaker is frosted, then strain into a chilled martini glass. Top with the Cava (don't top with Cava until the moment you're ready to serve). Garnish with the lemon peel and serve.

ACKNOWLEDGMENTS

To Suzanne O'Neill, my intrepid editor, whose thoughtful guidance brought the book into focus, one chapter at a time.

To Jessica, who makes it all possible and allows me to pretend that her great ideas are mine. *Thank you for this life we have together.*

To Gracie—a list of all the things I'm grateful for would take up an entire book, a book I would probably title *Cooking for Gracie.*

To Margot—at this stage of the game you pretty much own me. Time, thankfully, is on my side; the most rebellious thing you can do at this point is crawl in the other direction. I'm going to try to gain a little perspective as you grow older and will do my best to take the responsible-parent approach when you ask to borrow money for a three-day weekend in Vegas or suggest a semester abroad in Amsterdam.

To the nurses in the St. Luke's–Roosevelt neonatal intensive care unit, who gave so freely, taught so wisely, cared so deeply, and saw so clearly that the very thought of them gives me a lump in my throat. I'm talking about you, Rose.

To Dr. Barak Rosenn, who said the words we most needed to hear, when we most needed to hear them: "Let's be optimistic." Those words meant more to us than you can imagine.

To Dr. Jatinder Bhatia and Amy Gates, who so generously offered their time to discuss infant nutrition.

To Denise Landis, who tested the *New York Times* recipes and translated my muddle into clear and readable steps.

To Carolyn Lee, who tipped over that first domino.

To Diane Reverand, a cherished friend and trusted confidante, and Sol Slotnik, who once held Gracie for three hours without a rest.

To Nick Fox, who set this whole foodie thing in motion.

To Pat Gurosky, who crystallized the theme and was the first person to speak the title aloud.

To Tony Eprile, Jonathan Evison, Ben Loory, and James P. Othmer, four very talented writers who've made me feel less alone in this thing of ours.

To all you Fiction Filers.

To everyone at Amilyne's in Alton Bay.

To M.A., who taught me to write from the ground up.

To the friends and family who contributed their time and enthusiasm to helping test recipes: Kelly Parker (who, after Jessica, has tried more of these recipes than anyone), Sara Zarr, Judy Schwartz, Brendan Eprile, Tony Eprile, Geoff and Shalagh Blanck, Sara Lukens, Diane Reverand, Allison Gutstein, Sarah Perry, Nancy Dixon, Richard Dixon, Tim Dixon, Lisa Berlenbach, Greg MacGilpin, Melissa Macomber, Merrie Urquhart (and you're a rock star, Merrie, for making so many recipes), Joan and Clive Whent (you too, Joan), Eric and Rhoda Silverberg, Ellen and Andy Welch, John Blesso (a kindred soul in all things food-related)—and the others I've surely forgotten to include here. Thank you all so much.

And to you, dear reader, for sustaining the dream.

RECIPE INDEX

ABOUT THE AUTHOR

Keith Dixon was born in Durham, North Carolina, but was raised in Bellefonte, Pennsylvania. For high school he attended the George School, a Quaker school in Newtown, Pennsylvania.

He began writing fiction in 1992, while attending Hobart College in Geneva, New York, and continued writing after moving to New York City. In 1993 he was hired by the *New York Times*, first as a copy boy and later as a member of the page-layout staff. He currently works in the news technology department.

His first published short story, "Absolutes and Other Uncertainties," appeared in the literary magazine *Other Voices* in 1996, and his first novel, *Ghostfires*, was published in 2004, followed in 2007 by *The Art of Losing*. His second published short story, "Sanctum," appeared in *Knock* magazine in 2009.

In 2008, soon after the birth of his first daughter, Grace, Keith published his first food-writing article, "Racket in the Kitchen, Ruckus in the Crib," about space-challenged city parents learning to cook silently. This article, along with two other food-writing articles, later became the basis of *Cooking for Gracie.*

His wife, Jessica, received a dual master's degree in elementary and special education from Bank Street College of Education, and taught first and second grade at the Aaron School in midtown Manhattan. They were married in 2004 and have a second daughter, Margot, who was born in 2010.

About the Type

The text of this book was set in Bell, a Transitional typeface created for Monotype in 1931 and originally cut by Richard Austin in 1788 for John Bell's type foundry. When Bell's foundry closed down, the font migrated for decades under different names: "English Copperplate" at the American Riverside Press in 1792, then "Brimmer," and later "Mountjoye," until font designer Stanley Morrison restored the name again in 1931. Unique to Bell is its break from tradition for numerals: They are twothirds the height of the font's capitals and sit evenly on the line.